What Other

The stepmoms I know definitely need a few quiet enriching moments each day to refill their love tanks. This devotional is written by women who have been in your running shoes on this unique love marathon. May this help every stepmom "run in such a way as you (and your marriage and family) might win"!

Pam Farrel, author of 40 books including bestselling
Men are like Waffles, Women are like Spaghetti

Stepmoms have a unique role, and often need encouragement. *Quiet Moments for the Stepmom Soul* offers reassurance and reflection. Take heart, stepmoms, the transparency of these three women will not only point you toward a place of rest and hope but also help you navigate the challenges you face.

Georgia Shaffer, author of *Avoiding the 12 Relationship Mistakes Women Make*, PA, Licensed Psychologist and Christian Life Coach

As a sister stepmom I understand stepfamily complexities and a stepmom's need for quiet time with the Lord. *Quiet Moments for the Stepmom Soul* furnishes a wonderful format to receive peace and comfort from God's word. Stepmom to stepmom, I want to encourage you to allow the words on these pages to wash away your stress and fears. Let God, and these seasoned stepmoms, transform your marriage and stepfamily.

Janet Thompson, founder of Woman to Woman Mentoring, speaker and award-winning author of 18 books, including *Praying for Your Prodigal Daughter, Dear God, He's Home!,* and *Dear God, Why Can't I Have a Baby?*

Quiet Moments for the Stepmom Soul:

Encouragement for the Journey

Laura Petherbridge

Gayla Grace

Heather Hetchler

DEDICATION

We dedicate this devotional to all the women who are

dating, engaged to or married to a man with children.

We live in the stepfamily trenches with you.

We know your heart. We feel your hurt.

We pray the following pages bring hope to your soul and a quiet

place to rest.

Heather Hetchler   *Gayla Grace*   *Laura Petherbridge*

"Come with me by yourselves to a quiet place and get some rest"
(Mark 6:31 NIV).

CONTENTS

FOREWORD

Wish you had a support group of stepmoms you could call for encouragement, wisdom, and strength when you need it most? Most stepmoms do. Sitting and talking with trusted friends is ideal, but if you don't have that this book is the next best thing. *Quiet Moments for the Stepmom Soul* is your virtual support group with trusted friends. So, grab a cup of coffee and let Gayla, Heather, and Laura share their hearts with you.

— Ron L. Deal, bestselling author of *The Smart Stepfamily* and Director of FamilyLife Blended™

INTRODUCTION

To Our Sister Stepmoms:

We get it!! We know there are many days when you:

Need refuge for your weary soul.
Seek someone who truly understands.
Wonder if the stepmom journey is worth it.
Wish the biological mom would move far away.
Think you might be going crazy.
Are overwhelmed with feelings of loneliness and rejection in your own home.
Obsess over whether your own kids are suffering.
Long for one day ALONE with your spouse.
Long for one day ALONE with your kids.
Long for one day ALONE.
Feel like you've lost yourself.
Consider hiding under a pile of dirty laundry, no matter how smelly.
Believe God views you as a failure as a wife and stepmom.

We understand. Really, we do.
That's why we wrote this devotional.
It is the desire of our hearts that the words on these pages from three stepmoms who "get it" provide you with: encouragement, everyday insight, practical steps, relaxation, and a little laughter.

Grab a cappuccino or a sweet tea and take a few minutes to allow God's living Word and His lavish love to wash over you. May this devotional impart a fresh wind at your back, a holy nudge to your mind, and a gentle caress to your heart.

May you feel the love of God and the support of three stepmom sisters who live in the trenches with you and desire to bring encouragement to your soul.

Jesus Loves You. We understand you. You are not alone. It's a promise.

Laura Petherbridge   *Gayla Grace*   *Heather Hetchler*

Shocking Words

"Search me, O God, and know my heart; try me, and know my anxieties. And see if there is any wicked way in me, and lead me in the way everlasting" (Psalm 139:23-24 NKJV).

Thought for the Day: Just because I think it, doesn't mean I have to speak it.

Something happened shortly after I became a stepmom. My mouth started saying things I hadn't realized my mind was capable of thinking.

The negative thoughts that entered my mind and exited through my mouth shocked me. I was becoming someone I didn't like. Through prayer and introspection, I discovered I had many layers of hurt from my childhood and previous marriage that were being pricked by the challenges of stepfamily living. My struggles as a stepmother triggered emotions I hadn't dealt with previously.

Now, when negative thoughts come to mind, I try to stop and ask myself why and work through any underlying hurts or unrealistic expectations. I still have negative thoughts but my need to speak them has lessened.

Prayer: *Lord, search my heart for past hurts and help me work through them so I may control what I do with them instead of allowing them to control me. I want to turn to You with my pain instead of turning on someone else. Help me to replace negative thoughts with grateful thinking. Infuse my heart with a hunger for You.*

~ Heather

Perseverance Pays

"Let perseverance finish its work so that you may be mature and complete, not lacking anything" (James 1:4 NIV).

Thought for the Day: Persevering on tough days requires an intentional choice. It's a choice that comes with a reward.

My husband is a runner. He's completed dozens of marathons and half marathons across the country. As I've watched him train month after month, I've noticed he never talks about quitting. Even when it hurts. Even when it's hard.

The stepparenting journey reminds me of marathon training. If a marathoner begins a race with even a small consideration to quit when it gets hard, he won't finish. When the muscle cramps slow his gait, when the road stretches endlessly, when his breathing labors under the hot sun, as others stumble along the way — he has to decide he won't give in to the temptation to stop. The choice is daunting.

I find the same to be true as a stepparent. On days when I feel like an outsider in my own home or get snarly looks when my stepchild comes through the door, it's easy to think about quitting. But after two decades as a stepparent, I've learned the stepparenting journey is a marathon, not a sprint. On hard days, I make an intentional choice to persevere, refusing to consider thoughts of quitting. I'm reminded of James 1:12 that says, "A man who endures trials is blessed..." (HCSB).

Prayer: *Lord, I have days when I want to give up. But I've committed to stay for better or worse. Please give me hope on hard days and help me to persevere through the challenges.*

~ Gayla

Jesus Take the Wheel

"And yet, O Lord, You are our Father. We are the clay, and You are the potter. We all are formed by Your hand" (Isaiah 64:8 NLT).

Thought for the Day: I surrender all.

One of the benchmarks of Christian maturity is when I decide to let Jesus take the wheel. And that often means relinquishing control to others, including my husband.

Recently, Steve had a big decision to make that would significantly affect our future. I was concerned that he was allowing emotions regarding the complex situation to cloud his judgment. I'd watched him make this same mistake in the past, and I gently told him so. He listened. But I was fairly certain he wasn't going to do what I felt he should.

Normally, I would have continued to (translation: nag) remind him. But this time I took it to God. This allowed the Holy Spirit to press wisdom into my soul, "Laura, leave Steve alone with me. You have voiced your concerns, now let go. Trust him to me." Finally, I listened. I allowed God to be the Potter who molds me into what He wants me to be. A wife who stands beside her husband and voices an opinion, but without pushing, shoving, and badgering the poor guy. I stepped back and said, "I trust you, Steve. Whatever you decide, I'll stand by you."

How do you think that made him feel? Emotionally he transformed into Superman. Jill Briscoe explains it well, "Once we seek what God has in mind for us, then He begins to make us a vessel fit for glory. But we must be pliable. As the Potter works the clay, He continually wets it. If he doesn't, it gets dry and becomes a misshapen lump, good for nothing."[1]

Becoming like Christ is a daily surrender, but it gets easier when I realize His pottery hands and wheel are mightier than my problems.

---

[1] Jill Briscoe, *Everyday Matters Bible for Women*, Hendrickson Publishers Marketing, LLC, Peabody Massachusetts, 2012, p875

Prayer: *Precious Lord, I desire to fully trust You with my day-to-day decisions. I want to be moldable instead of dry and crusty. Make me like Christ, a willing servant who listens to Your wisdom. Then I will be equipped to know when to speak, act or respond, and when to keep silent. Thank you for Your patience with me. I love You, Lord.*

~ Laura

Are You Lonesome Tonight?

"Be strong and courageous. Do not be afraid or terrified because of them, for the LORD your God goes with you; He will never leave you nor forsake you" (Deuteronomy 31:6 NIV).

Thought for the Day: You are never alone with God who anchors your soul.

Loneliness. It's the last emotion I anticipated feeling when I married a man with two kids. Yet after saying "I do," it was the emotion that hit me hardest. As a married woman, with a blended family of eight, I felt lonelier than I had as a single mom of four.

When my stepdaughters were around, I felt unwanted. They made it clear they wanted their dad to themselves. When my kids were gone to their father's house and it was just me and my husband with his two girls, my heart would sink. My husband wanted me to do things with them, yet I felt lonely knowing my presence wasn't welcomed by my stepdaughters.

About a year into our marriage, my husband bought me a comfortable chair for our bedroom where I could go and read when I felt sad. While it was a kind gesture, it made me feel even more disconnected. I remember sitting in that chair and crying to God how lonely I was. But as I cried the words out loud, I realized that with God, I am never alone.

I was looking to feel connected by the relationships in my life when there is really only one person who can make me feel complete—God. In the song "You Won't Let Go," Michael W. Smith sings about how our Lord is the anchor of our soul—He will not let go. Jesus will never leave or forsake us. Take a moment to let that soak in. You are never alone!

Prayer: *Dear Heavenly Father, I seek You. In those dark moments when I allow myself to believe I am all alone, help me remember because of You, I am never alone. You are the anchor of my soul and You hold me tight. I pray that I never forget how You hold me and love me. Help me not to let my struggles or feelings of being unwanted cloud my thoughts. May I find peace and rest in You and know that I am never alone. Thank you, Jesus, for filling me and walking with me.*

~ Heather

Live Fearlessly

"For the Spirit God gave us does not make us timid, but gives us power, love and self-discipline" (2 Timothy 1:7 NIV).

Thought for the Day: God gives us a spirit of power.

Her swollen eyes told the story. Tears began as the stepmom started to speak. "Why is this so hard? My stepchildren are adults. We rarely see them, but when we do, hurtful words fly."

Whether stepchildren are young or old, stepfamily adjustments exist. Unhealed wounds of the past can drive stepchildren to intimidate and alienate a stepparent from the family circle. The old adage, "Hurt people hurt people" rang true for this stepmom's stepdaughter.

It takes a spirit of power from God to reach out after hurtful daggers have been thrown our way. Fear can cripple our ability to respond. But this stepmom chose to continue to reach out in compassion, and her adult stepdaughter eventually began to accept her gestures of love.

I love the story of David and Goliath (1 Samuel 17). David's faith that the Lord would walk with him through the battle gave him the confidence to fight Goliath, a giant of tremendous size and strength, and win.

The same holds true for us. We gain confidence to walk fearlessly in our stepmom role when we claim the spirit of power God gives us and believe He will walk with us into battle.

Prayer: *Heavenly Father, I want to live fearlessly in my stepmom role. I can't do it alone. I claim Your promise today that I've been given a spirit of power. I need that power – the power that only You can give. Thank you that I can rest in Your promise.*

~ Gayla

Can I Run Away From Home?

"Jesus understands every weakness of ours, because He was tempted in every way that we are. But He did not sin!" (Hebrews 4:15 CEV).

Thought for the Day: This is not what I bargained for. Fortunately, God understands.

"If I knew then, what I know now, I wouldn't have entered this marriage," two-year stepmom Julie stated. (Have you whispered these words too? Take heart, precious stepmom — it's normal.)
It's very common to have thoughts of marriage regret — I did. It had nothing to do with my love for Steve. I wanted to escape the unexpected frustration, anxiety, shock, and drama associated with stepfamily living.

That's when I knew I couldn't do it on my own strength. This would require supernatural, Jesus-sized, over-the-top love, compassion, wisdom and grace. And I didn't possess, or even desire, those characteristics when it came to my stepfamily.
Fortunately, that's God's specialty. He loves making all things new. He loves transforming my weakness into His strength. He shines while doing spiritual CPR on an exhausted, despondent heart.

All He waits on is my willingness to hand it over to Him. Corrie ten Boom, who survived the Nazi concentration camps, is one of my all-time favorite Christian women. She advises, "Trying to do the Lord's work in your own strength is the most confusing, exhausting, and tedious of all work. But when you are filled with the Holy Spirit, then the ministry of Jesus just flows out of you."[2]

Prayer: *Lord, I admit I've thought about leaving this marriage. It's too difficult. I'm drained. No matter how hard I try, it doesn't seem to get better. And yet — I made a vow, a commitment. Not just to my husband but to You. The desire of my heart is to honor You. So I lay it all down, Jesus. I come to You. I don't know how to survive in this marriage. But You do. I trust You.*

~ Laura

---

[2] Corrie Ten Boom, *Anywhere Her Leads Me*, Compiled by Judith Couchman 1997, Servant Publications, Ann Arbor MI

Putting Down the Stepmom Shovel

"The LORD is near to the brokenhearted and saves those who are crushed in spirit" (Psalm 34:18 NIV).

Thought for the Day: You didn't put the hole in your stepchild's heart. You can't fill it.

When you care about someone, it is hard to watch them hurt. When I said "I do" to a full-time father with two girls, I had my love goggles superglued to my face. Naively, I thought the love I had for my husband and his daughters would be enough to help me mother them. I believed my well-meaning heart could take away my stepdaughters' pain.

As we started our life together, it seemed the more I did for my two stepdaughters, the more they pushed me away. I remember going all out for my youngest stepdaughter's sixth birthday (the same as I do for my biological children). She gave me the silent treatment all day. Afterward, she told me that she hated how I'd made a big deal for her birthday because she wanted it to be her mom doing it. "I'm not even your kid and you do all this. Why can't it be my own mom?" she screamed in tears. Then it clicked—I hadn't made the hole in her heart and I couldn't fill it.

When I truly got that her pain was her pain and I couldn't take it away, a light went on and a weight was lifted. Now I try to give my stepkids consistent care, direction and love regardless of what mood they are in, without any expectations. When times get tough, I'm the parent they turn to. I do what is right because it's right, not to get a thank you from them.

Prayer: *Dear Heavenly Father, my heart desires to walk alongside my husband to help parent his children. They come from a place of pain and it's pain I didn't cause. Help me to cover these kids in prayer and place my trust in You that all will be worked together for their good. May I let go of my need to fix things and cling to Your promises of hope and peace.*

~ Heather

Stepfamily Bonds

"Consider it a great joy, my brothers, whenever you experience various trials, knowing that the testing of your faith produces endurance" (James 1:2-3 HCSB).

Thought for the Day: A struggling relationship doesn't spell failure. It takes time for stepfamilies to grow together and bond.

"I feel like I've failed." The new stepmom's words surprised me. "There's so much tension in our home with ongoing struggles between my daughter and my stepdaughter, and constant disagreements with my husband on how to parent. This is much harder than I imagined."

I began to reminiscence of our early years. They were full of tension also. Power struggles with my husband on how to parent, unhappy kids vying for my attention, combative ex-spouses, and personal insecurities as a stepparent contributed to stress-filled days. I remember longing for single parenting days again when I had only to concern myself with my two daughters.

Relief washed over me one day when I learned that stepfamily experts say it takes four to seven years for relationships to come together and begin to bond. We were normal! I didn't have to blame myself for the tension in our home.

I encouraged the new stepmom to relax her expectations while her family worked through the kinks in their relationships.

Prayer: *Heavenly Father, please give me patience as our stepfamily relationships come together. Show me how to do my part to create a loving environment in our home.*

~ Gayla

If I'm Happy, My Kids Are Happy — Right?

"Five of them were foolish, and five were wise" (Matthew 25:2 NLT).

Thought for the Day: The couple views remarriage as a new chance at love. The kids — not so much.

Divorce brings with it a kaleidoscope of emotions.

For example, Mom and Dad divorce. Dad is very sad and depressed because he didn't want the divorce. A few months later he meets a wonderful woman and he falls "head over heels" in love. He begins acting like a teenager with a goofy smile on his face 24/7.

Life is good — again.

He thinks to himself, "After feeling as though life was over, I'm breathing again. I'm crazy in love with a fabulous woman who makes me feel alive. Surely, this will be a great thing for my kids. I know they want me to be happy. They will definitely love this woman as much as I do. If I'm happy they will be happy — right?"

Wrong.

Dad views his new relationship as another chance for love; the kids often see it as one more loss. To them Dad is absorbed in a new person, (and her kids if she has them), and they fear they will get pushed out of the family photo.

When forming a stepfamily it's important to understand that it takes time and hard work to merge into a solid unit. Kids (young or old) normally do want a parent to be happy. But their perspective on how that should look might be vastly different than the parent assumes.

Prayer: *Holy God, help me to recognize that kids of divorce have a different perspective than the parents. Show me how to understand the emotion behind attitudes. Remind me that what I observe happening on the outside, is merely a reflection of the hurting process on in the inside.*

~ Laura

Learning My Control Panel

"Do not conform to the pattern of this world, but be transformed by the renewing of your mind. Then you will be able to test and approve what God's will is — His good, pleasing and perfect will" (Romans 12:2 NIV).

Thought for the Day: Use your time and talent to control the only person you can — You!

Sometimes I don't realize I'm trying to control a situation. I dive right in with a heart to help and end up feeling hurt when my guidance is rejected.

It is so apparent I have no control over what unfolds day to day in my stepfamily. And even while I understand this truth, I still sometimes allow the drama to wear me down.

I believe my true need is not to control, but rather to be understood and valued. I know these two needs can only be completely fulfilled through God, yet there are days when I forget and I try and get them from my spouse and kids.

I am determined to seek God to feel understood, valued, loved, and validated. Just as I am human and I will fail my husband and kids, so they, too, will fail me. The best way for me to control a situation is to put God in control of it and then trust Him completely. Some days I'll like the stepfamily journey and other days I will not. Regardless of the waves or calm in my life, my heart seeks to worship Him and give Him thanks.

Prayer: *Dear Lord, my burdens are heavy. Some days I feel crushed beneath them. I will turn to You for comfort and peace. I recognize my burdens will not disappear, but my head and my heart will be filled with the One who is always in control. Heavenly Father, help me feel peace. I ask You to gift me with discernment. Guide me away from trying to control. Fill me. You are enough. I seek to live that. I will search for joy in Your unwavering love and comfort, and not in the details of my day.*

~ Heather

The Value of a Flexible Spirit

"Do all things without complaining and disputing" (Philippians 2:14 NKJV).

Thought for the Day: With God's help, I have power to control my emotions and my behavior.

My head began to pound as I drove to the dreaded doctor's appointment with our youngest son. My day of deadlines and conference calls didn't include time to wait on a doctor triple-booked in the middle of flu season. But when our son missed another day of school due to dizziness and headaches, I sensed an urgency to seek a doctor's opinion.

I took a deep breath as we walked into the standing room only waiting area. I imagined my blood pressure would soon skyrocket from the germ-infested room of screaming kids. I quickly realized I had a choice to make. Would I seek God's help to settle my nerves and take control of my emotions and behavior or begin a downward spiral of negativity?

The stepmom journey often includes unplanned events. When an irresponsible ex-spouse fails to show up again, or a stepchild leaves his school project at the other parent's house across town, how will we react? We can gripe about the aggravating change to our day and perpetuate a negative spirit toward those around us, or we can ask for God's help to maintain a flexible attitude.

The doctor reported an excessive amount of fluid in both ears that contributed to my son's dizziness that day. A steroid shot and new prescriptions were administered and we headed home. My son began to feel better immediately and I prided myself on going against my natural tendency to complain and instead, sought God's help to take control of my emotions in the midst of a busy day.

Prayer: *Heavenly Father, I like order to my days, but that isn't always possible on the stepmom journey. Help me maintain a flexible attitude when unplanned events surface.*

~ Gayla

The Walking Wounded

"And the one sitting on the throne said, "See, I am making all things new!" (Revelation 21:5 TLB).

Thought for the Day: Have I allowed God to heal my past?

When we see a child hurting, especially when the wound is due to the poor choices of a parent or family member, it can trigger a stepmom's hidden emotional pain.

Stepmom Marcia shares, "My stepdaughter cries when her mom doesn't show up at her dance recitals. It makes me furious. And then a tidal wave of my own memories hit and in my mind I'm a little girl again anxiously awaiting my daddy to show up at my gymnastics competitions. It's as though remembering my own pain sends a surge of grief, sadness, and abandonment that sweeps over me."

I understand. God used this same scenario as a way of revealing my own emotional wounds. In order to become a stable stepmom, I had to get help for my own childhood pain.

This required professional counseling, attending retreats and support groups, praying with godly women, discovering and memorizing Bible verses that spoke to my pain and reading Christian resources written by those who understood. (Ex: *Praying God's Word* by Beth Moore, *The Search for Significance* by Robert S. McGee, *Healing For Damaged Emotions* by David Seamands and *Waking the Dead* by John Eldredge).

Is it time for you to do the same?

Prayer: *Lord, I try to ignore or deny all the ugly stuff in my past, but the truth is I've never really dealt with it. I'm still dragging it behind and inside of me. Thank you for using my stepfamily to uproot those roots of fear, pain and anger. Heal me, Oh God. You are the Great Physician of my body, soul, mind and emotions. Amen.*

~ Laura

Become a Blessing Detective

"Whoever seeks good finds favor, but evil comes to one who searches for it" (Proverbs 11:27 NIV).

Thought for the Day: Gratitude opens our hearts to God and enables us to feel peace regardless of our circumstances.

During a very cold winter, my husband and I decided to take our six children to Florida for spring break. It was a true leap of faith as past vacations had proved that a family vacation is typically not a vacation at all. With the cold temps, this time we were sure the kids would love a trek to a warmer climate. We were wrong.

I was sitting on the beach the second day listening to the kids complaining. I was allowing the negative tape in my head to play about how the kids didn't appreciate family outings when I noticed something. My oldest stepdaughter was holding my youngest daughter's hand and walking her out of the ocean. My daughter had taken in a huge gulp of sea water and her big step-sis helped her to shore. That turned out to be one of the greatest blessings of the trip for me.

Thinking about it later, I realized when I changed my focus and looked for the blessings, I found many. Yes, there had been a lot of complaining, but there was some great stuff too. My sons helped carry their sisters' luggage. My daughter shared food with her stepsister. The kids learned to negotiate and decide together who would sit where and what they wanted to do.

Vacations are stressful regardless what type of family you have, but if you look hard you can find—and more importantly, treasure—the blessings. In life, there is a mix of blessings and burdens. What we focus on determines our mood and our perception of our family. We will always have struggles, but we will always have blessings, and that is what I choose to focus on.

Prayer: *Dear Heavenly Father, open my eyes to the blessings of our family. When I allow myself to dwell on the negatives, please convict me and remind me of the good being built. Lord, I want You to focus on the good in me so help me to focus on the good in each of my family members and on the big and small blessings in our lives.*

~ Heather

The Beauty of Humility

"Be completely humble and gentle; be patient, bearing with one another in love" (Ephesians 4:2 NIV).

Thought for the Day: A humble heart opens the door to meaningful relationships.

Taking on the role of stepmom had been harder than I anticipated, and I didn't always get it right. I wanted my stepchildren to know I cared deeply for them, although I didn't show it well. I felt the need to apologize for my imperfect efforts of years' past as a stepmom.

I treasured their reactions. My stepson immediately expressed compassion and apologized for his part in making it difficult for me, recognizing he hadn't been easy to raise. My stepdaughter offered kind remarks toward me also, negating my need to apologize. After several years together as a stepfamily, my stepchildren understood my desire to love and treat them well. Unfortunately, my behavior didn't always coincide.

More important than my apology, my humble heart helped my stepchildren recognize my effort toward good relationships. It didn't gloss over every harsh word or sweep away hard seasons we'd had together. But it offered a new beginning toward a future that included love and respect for one another.

Eating humble pie is never easy. It requires a daily walk with the Lord that allows Him to show us our errant ways. It takes courage to follow through when we don't know the reaction we'll receive from others. But a humble heart opens the door to sincere, meaningful relationships.

Prayer: *Heavenly Father, You know my heart. I want to follow Your ways that include a humble and gentle spirit but I need Your help. Give me the courage to respond to my stepchildren with a Christ-like heart.*

~ Gayla

NO Loitering!

"See, I will create new heavens and a new earth. The former things will not be remembered, nor will they come to mind" (Isaiah 65:17 NIV).

Thought for the Day: I may be concealing past pain without realizing it.

"I had no idea I was still carrying so much fear and baggage from my first marriage until you asked me about our financial stress," Emma stated.

"I didn't realize I had pushed the memory from my mind until this moment," she revealed. "But as we talked, all of a sudden I could see my ex-husband standing in the kitchen saying to me, 'I'm leaving. You are on your own to take care of these four kids. Don't expect me to help you—because I'm not.' And he walked out the door. I stood there in shock. I was a stay-at-home-mom. How would I provide for my children?"

During a life coaching session, Emma, Gary, and I were discussing the financial clashes they were having. They were amazed to discover that the issues had little to do with money.

Emma's first husband abandoned her. Gary's first wife drove them deeply into debt.

They weren't facing a financial crisis, but rather a "Ghost of ex-spouse past." And neither of them realized it, until I posed a few probing questions that brought hidden fears and concerns to the surface.

Most people think they heal and recover from past wounds quickly. But that's rare. And just like this couple, the toxic fumes from relationships past can lurk under the relationship seeping poison into the marriage.

Look beyond the ex-wife in law, the inflammatory comments from your stepkids, your husband's unwillingness to address his children, your loneliness, the frustration of being a stepmom, and go deeper. Much deeper.

Like this couple, it might require a third party to unleash the dragon hiding in the recesses of your mind. I assure you, addressing the pain of the past, brings healing to the future.

Prayer: *Lord, I want to know if I have unhealed areas in my heart and mind. Show me how to discover if there is any brokenness still prowling in my soul. I know it may be hard to hear or face, but I trust You. I believe without complete healing I can't move forward. Heal my past, so that I can glorify You with my future.*

~ Laura

Encourage One Another

"Therefore comfort each other and edify one another, just as you also are doing" (1 Thessalonians 5:11 NKJV).

Thought for the Day: There is a sense of strength that comes from knowing you are not alone. Find your stepmom tribe for encouragement, support and inspiration.

Natalie, a stepmom of three years, wrote me asking to be connected with another stepmom in her area. She was fighting feelings of isolation, wondering if she was going crazy. None of her friends were stepmoms and, therefore, did not relate to her struggles.

This stepmom's desire to connect with other stepmothers is a common one. Natalie wasn't looking for someone to solve her problems, but to validate her hurts and encourage her on the journey.

Early in my marriage, I began to question my emotions. When I shared with my husband how his youngest child treated me when he wasn't around, he told me I was making too much of it and to be "the adult." Years later, he admitted he hadn't wanted to see the negativity in his own child. "No one wants to believe their child deceives," he said.

Just like Natalie, I desired to feel validated in my experiences. I needed a processing partner, and it wasn't my husband. It was another stepmom who understood and encouraged me and my marriage.

Prayer: *Dear Heavenly Father, thank you for the gift of stepmom sisters. Lord, You know my situation. Please bring stepmom friends into my life and help me to nurture these relationships. I seek to learn from women who have come before me as well as to share and help those women just starting out. God, may I feel Your touch through the love of stepmom sisters who understand and encourage me and my marriage.*

~ Heather

Don't Wait to Get Help

"Walk with the wise and become wise, for a companion of fools suffers harm" (Proverbs 13:20 NIV).

Thought for the Day: Seek help for struggling relationships.

When we were dating, my soon-to-be husband and I often talked about the challenges we faced—how to parent each other's children, stepsibling rivalry, co-parenting with ex-spouses, and combining two households. We knew there would be adjustments, but we thought we could simply love our kids through whatever came along.

We were wrong.

We learned that blending families, especially when there are children from both sides, requires more than love. It takes tenacity, patience, faithfulness, thick skin, compromising attitudes, a willingness to go the distance when you want to quit, and so much more. I had no idea what I was signing up for when I said, "I do."

Just a few months into our marriage, we realized we needed help. Serious help. We were seeking the Lord for answers but needed someone to guide us through everyday challenges. We found a professional counselor who understood stepfamily dynamics. He gave us insight into why we responded defensively or held onto a stubborn spirit when we parented and how to change it. He helped us work through hurt and anger and find forgiveness for one another.

If you reach an impasse in your stepfamily relationships, don't wait to seek help. Stepfamily life is complicated and often requires an objective person to help you wade through the muck.

Prayer: *Dear Lord, I have issues every day I don't know how to handle. Please give me wisdom as I parent someone else's child. Show me where to turn to find healthy answers to my stepfamily dilemmas. Thank you for walking with us.*

~ Gayla

Changing the View

"But I know this: I was blind, and now I can see!" (John 9:25b NLT).

Thought for the Day: A new perspective can change the outcome.

Recently a pastor shared that he and his wife were strolling through an art gallery when she stopped in front of a masterpiece and commented, "Isn't it beautiful?" Tilting his head, his thoughts were more along the line, "Is it upside down?"

This is a great example of two people looking at the same thing, and seeing two completely different images.

As a stepmom it's advisable to take a peek through a lens other than your own. I recommend stepping into your stepchild's viewpoint. This is when growing up in a stepfamily can provide an advantage.

I experienced my Dad's remarriage at age thirteen. I liked the woman he married, she was nice to me. But afterward I didn't see him as much. And when I did, the time with my dad was shared with her two sons. This didn't seem fair at all.

Her sons, my stepbrothers, got to have my father every day—all day. I only got him for a few hours every other week.

As a stepmom, we often want everyone to merge into one big family. And often it's advisable to do things together. But doesn't your position change when you evaluate the situation through my childhood eyes? Can you see why a child of divorce can become resentful, jealous, or nasty toward the stepfamily dynamic?

Give your stepchild a gift. It's a sacrifice, but offering your stepchild time alone with his or her Daddy is wise. In the end it will benefit the marriage more than you'll ever know.

Prayer: *Lord, I admit — I'm selfish. With work, school activities, and other commitments I see so little of my husband. I don't want him to spend more time away from me. And yet I know his children need him too. Help me to let go of my desire to control everything. And show me how to have a healthy stepfamily that meets the essential needs of each family member. I believe You love us. Thank you ahead of time.*

~ Laura

Stretched Thin

"Let us not become weary in doing good, for at the proper time we will reap a harvest if we do not give up" (Galatians 6:9 NIV).

Thought for the Day: You are going to be stretched, but you can do it.

If you grew up in the 70s or 80s you are probably familiar with the popular toy, Stretch Armstrong. This action figure's most notable feature is its ability to be stretched from 15 inches to four or five feet then back to its original shape.

Through stepfamily life, God stretches you in ways you never imagined.

A stepmom is stretched thin living with a stepchild she doesn't trust.

A stepmom is stretched thin dealing with an ex-spouse who has control over her schedule and finances without her consent.

A stepmom is stretched thin _____ (fill in with your biggest struggle).

Day to day, I can't anticipate how God will stretch me. One minute, He asks me to respond in love to a stepchild who is difficult to be around. The next, He calls me to be a peacemaker with an ex-spouse. He calls me to love and respect my husband even when I don't agree with his parenting decisions. Ugh. This is hard.

No matter how far I am stretched each day, God returns me to center. However, unlike Stretch who goes back to his original size, I am changed. God is rooting out my need to control (that I never knew I had); He is filling me with trust in Him, which makes it easier to be stretched because I know it's for my own good. I'm trusting Him to say where He wants me to go and what He wants me to say. I seek to do the things God stretches me to do because He is calling me to do them. In my flesh, I am weak and have my own ideas. But through Him, I am able to be strong.

Prayer: *Dear Heavenly Father, every day brings different challenges and different blessings. As I'm pulled in many different directions, may I always pull myself close to You. May I be centered in Your truths as I strive to be a godly wife, stepmom and friend. Throughout my day, I will keep my eyes focused on You, Lord, so I don't measure my worth by the words of others, but by the truth of who I am in You.*

~ Heather

Give Up Perfection

"Whatever you do, work at it with all your heart, as working for the Lord, not for human masters" (Colossians 3:23 NIV).

Thought for the Day: I'm blessed even when life isn't perfect.

I'm a recovering perfectionist. I like my house clean. I like my closet organized. I'm easily annoyed by clutter. I like the dishes done and laundry put away. I could go on and on.

My perfectionism spilled over into unrealistic expectations of my new stepmom role. If I were Super Stepmom my stepchildren would love me. If I did everything right, we would be one, big, happy family.

Unfortunately, that didn't happen. I couldn't force relationships to bond or make my stepchildren love me overnight. When I finally lowered my expectations and gave up perfectionism, life got easier for me (and those I lived with).

I began to focus on doing my work for the Lord. I wanted to please God, not men. If I did the role God called me to do to the best of my ability, I wasn't responsible for the outcome—God was. I didn't have to worry if our stepfamily took two steps backward instead of a step forward. I placed our stepfamily in God's hands, and asked Him to take the reins. That gave me more energy to "work at it with all your heart."

I found freedom as I let go of my perfectionistic ways. And my family discovered a wife, mom, and stepmom they wanted to hang out with more often.

Prayer: *Dear Lord, I want to please You today. Show me how to lower my expectations and let go of my perfectionistic ways. Help me to trust You with the end result.*

~ Gayla

The Money Monster

"It is better to live right and be poor than to be sinful and rich" (Psalm 37:16 CEV).

Thought for the Day: Ignoring financial stress doesn't make it go away.

Handling money in a second marriage can be extremely challenging because there is often financial baggage from the first marriage.

"Two-thirds of all remarried couples have financial issues that are tied to their past relationships. Debt, bills, settlements are among the top relationship issues for remarried couples."[3]

As a stepmom it's easy for resentment to build. I remember working in a highly stressful medical job. Doctors barked demeaning orders at me all day. It felt like I labored in vain, while my hard-earned money went to pay for my husband's ex-wife-in-law.

God helped me change the perspective.

I prayed to see the money from another standpoint. First, I saw the child support paying the rent. They had to have shelter. In the frigid western New York climate it was easy to view the money as paying their heating bill.

When the ex-wife uses money as a weapon to frustrate the stepmom's home, or manipulate the Dad, it can create a division in the marriage. God can and will reveal how to stand by the divorce agreement while not allowing the former spouse to rob your joy.

With a new lens it can become easier to shake off the anger and resentment associated with stepfamily finances.

Remember, God owns it all. Our job is to learn how to be good caretakers (stewards) of the money and possessions He has entrusted to us. When we are obedient with our part, He is faithful with His part.

---

[3] Ron L. Deal and David H Olson, *The Remarriange Checkup: Tools to Help Your Marriage Last a Lifetime* (Bloomington, NM: Bethany Housee, 2010), p 203.

Prayer: *Holy God, help me to remember that I own nothing. You own it all. Everything I have is on loan to me. I take none of it with me when I die. Teach us how to manage our finances in a way that glorifies and honors You. Where we have accumulated debt, show us how to begin paying it off. And give us the discipline to do what it takes to become free from the money monster.*

~ Laura

Desiring My Husband

"Keep your heart with all vigilance, for from it flow the springs of life" (Proverbs 4:23 ESV).

Thought for the Day: Ask God to keep your heart soft toward your husband and to place within you a desire for him that burns deeply.

There are days when I feel distant from my husband. There have been seasons in our marriage when I've felt disconnected from him for more than a few days.

Learning to step back from the challenges of stepfamily life without detaching myself from the man I love is a work in progress. As a woman, my feelings are all tangled together and I have to be both prayerful and intentional not to allow my struggles in our family to impact how connected I feel toward my spouse and our marriage. I have to admit, when my husband and I are not getting along, the last thing I want to do is to be intimate with him.

One time I asked him, "How can you be upset with me at 5pm and want to make love five hours later?"

He replied, "Because I love you and the fact that we disagree doesn't impact that. I don't think of it as make-up sex, but rather re-bonding."

Understanding my husband's perspective coupled with God's command to enjoy each other has brought renewed intimacy even during the tough times.

Prayer: *Lord, help me to stay connected to my husband physically, emotionally, and spiritually. When my flesh wants to be in a different room, convict me to come back to center with him. I love him, God, and I acknowledge that when things are tough it can be challenging to want to be with him. Keep our desire for one another burning brightly. Keep my heart soft toward him and help him to treat me with a Christ-like love.*

~ Heather

Note, if you are in an emotionally and/or physically abusive relationship please know that the above does not pertain to you. Please seek counseling and keep you and your children safe.

Compassion Binds Relationships

"Because of the LORD's great love we are not consumed, for his compassions never fail. They are new every morning; great is Your faithfulness" (Lamentations 3:22-23 NIV).

Thought for the Day: When we look at life through the lens of our stepchildren, we gain compassion toward them.

As my stepdaughter walked through the door from her mom's house with a downcast look, I imagined how she felt. The sadness of leaving her mom for a week must tug at her heart. The back and forth routine between two homes would be exhausting. Anxiety at our house with a new stepmom and two stepsisters could be intimidating. I began to think about how I could help her settle in on transition days.

I might not exactly understand the road my stepchildren walk, but I can empathize when they display troubled emotions. As I look at life through their lens, I gain compassion toward them.

Before joining our family, my stepchildren endured divorce of their parents at an early age. When their dad remarried, they suddenly had a stepmom and two stepsisters living in their home. I suspect that must have been quite an adjustment! When I began to consider the changes their young lives had experienced, I more easily found compassion for unstable emotions and disagreeable attitudes.

When we consider how the Lord offers new compassion toward us every morning, we realize our call to do the same for our stepchildren. As stepmoms, we have needs and wants too. However, if we keep our eyes solely focused on ourselves, we miss the chance to offer compassion to a hurting soul.

Prayer: *Dear Lord, my stepchildren have endured significant loss. Take away my selfish thoughts and give me compassion and empathy on difficult days. Help keep my eyes focused on You.*

~ Gayla

When Will I Be Loved?

"The Lord appeared to him from afar, saying, 'I have loved you with an everlasting love; Therefore I have drawn you with loving-kindness'" (Jeremiah 31:3 NASB).

Thought for the Day: Jesus loves me, this I know.

Right now I'm life coaching two stepmoms. One is forty-eight, the other is seventy-seven. The younger has adolescent stepkids and has been married for nine years. The senior stepmom has adult stepchildren from a thirty-seven year remarriage.

They live in different states separated by hundreds of miles. They are in completely different seasons of their lives, and yet they both have the exact same issue. Stepfamily stress is causing huge conflict and division in their marriages.

They want what any woman wants from a marriage—a husband who cherishes his wife. Weeping and lonely, they don't know what to do.

Although professional help is definitely needed, and boundaries must be set in place for the relationships to continue, there is a deeper issue.

It's crucial for these two women, and stepmoms everywhere, to understand that no man, woman or child can fill a God-sized void. God created us to obtain our identity and significance through Him, not people (including a husband), job, money, beauty or fame.

These women are exquisite. But until they see themselves as God does, their emptiness will continue. Our value comes from the Creator, the One who placed us here, the One who loved us enough to sacrifice Himself so that we could spend eternity with Him. He says we are precious, loved, treasured and adored.

Do you believe Him?

Prayer: *Dear God, I'm having a hard time believing I'm lovable. Everything around me screams that I'm a dreadful failure. Give me the eyes and perspective to see myself as You see me. Your love tells me I'm magnificently created. I'm delightfully cherished. I'm charmingly winsome. Help me to believe the truth, instead of lies.*

~ Laura

Seek a Peace-Filled Heart Not a Perfect Home

"Let the peace of Christ rule in your hearts, since as members of one body you were called to peace. And be thankful" (Colossians 3:15 NIV).

Thought for the Day: Let go of chasing a perfect home and focus on having a peace-filled heart.

I once joked with a friend that if she could look in my windows she might decide to sneak into my house, pack my bags and move me out. By the world's standards, I should be a mess with all the "stuff" my husband and I manage in our stepfamily. But I'm not. While my trials are many, my heart feels peace from the One who holds me tight.

Life is messy. Stepfamily life is beyond messy. Yet it is possible to feel joy that transcends the chaos swirling around you. My life is far from perfect but it is filled with peace because I choose to fill my head and heart with God's Word and promises.

God knows I'm nearest to perfection when I'm on my knees, and that is where I spend a lot of my time. I start every day in God's Word. Before checking social media or reading anything else, I read His words. Sometimes it is the Bible, other times a devotional. On mornings where the day seems to start ahead of me, I simply read a single verse or passage. But I always choose to start each day with God.

Beginning each day soaking in His Word makes a huge difference in my life. God's wisdom and hope brings peace to my heart even in the midst of a chaos-filled home.

My life is far from perfect, but it is filled with peace because I choose to fill my head and heart with Christ. We can't control the people in our home or the drama they bring into it, but we can control what we bring — a Christ-like attitude and a heart filled with God's peace.

Prayer: *Dear Heavenly Father, I seek to fill my heart and head with peace. I let go of chasing a perfect home or portraying a perfect family. You call me to follow You and to love others, not to be perfect. I will fill my head with Your Word and feel the peace only You can place in my heart.*

~ Heather

32

Don't Take it Personally

"Turn from evil and do good; seek peace and pursue it" (Psalm 34:14 NIV).

Thought for the Day: It's not all about me. I don't have to take others' behavior personally.

Baffled by my teenage son's behavior, I stood speechless as he slammed the door in my face. Usually a mild-mannered, easy-going kid, his outburst of anger surprised me. Had I done something to offend him? I quickly rehearsed our conversation in my head but couldn't determine the root of his anger.

I've learned a few things in the midst of raising five teenagers. Sometimes they have bad days—just like we do. Their behavior likely has nothing to do with us!

How often do we take things personally when our stepchild looks at us crossways or snarls at our innocent question about homework? I remember doing it in my younger years as a stepmom, particularly with my adolescent stepchildren. I didn't recognize the influence of raging hormones and teenage insecurities that contributed to out-of-control behavior.

When my son calmed down, I dared to enter his room and find out the cause of his meltdown. In tears, he relayed his difficult day at school and cutting remarks from a friend on the bus. I acknowledged his pain and asked how I could help. Before I left, I counseled him on the value of self-control and the consequences for lack of it. Then I reminded him of God's unending love for him, even on bad days.

If you're in the midst of raising teen stepchildren, dive beneath the surface of emotions you see. You'll likely find an insecure soul looking for identity and affirmation during difficult years.

Prayer: *Dear Lord, please refocus my thinking when it goes off course. Teach me how to pursue peace with those around me. Help me keep my thoughts on You and not take others' behavior personally.*

~ Gayla

I Was Wrong

"Wash away all my iniquity and cleanse me from my sin. For I know my transgressions, and my sin is always before me" (Psalm 51: 2-3 NIV).

Thought for the Day: Confession is good for the soul... and other things.

"You aren't my mother, you can't tell me what to do," the fourteen-year-old stepdaughter screamed.

"I thank God that I'm not your mother, you are a selfish brat," the stepmom quipped in reply.

And stepmoms everywhere hang their heads in humiliation and reply, "Ugh!! I've done that. I'm embarrassed to admit it but I have said something horrible to my stepchild." There's hardly a stepmom alive who isn't sorry for something she has said or done. It's the response after the mistake that separates a smart stepmom, from a selfish stepmom.

When the haunting discomfort of words better left unsaid is pressing hard on the mind, it's time to own up "I was wrong."

In today's scripture verse, King David reveals true repentance. He doesn't make excuses, or blame anyone else for his sin. He owns it.

Humbly admitting a poor choice to a stepchild can be more difficult than confessing to a biological child. A blood bond comes with forgiveness and loyalties that are often not offered to a stepmom. This places the stepmom in a vulnerable position. The stepchild (and possibly your spouse) might hold onto the offense as ammunition and throw the mistake back in the stepmom's face. With a biological child there is an eagerness to reunite and forgive a parent when wrongdoing occurs. They desire a restoration that may not be true with a stepparent.

Even though the risks are higher, and a stepmom might not reap the rewards immediately, it's necessary to ask for forgiveness. God sees your heart and knows your motives, even when no one else does. The bridge to a stepchild's heart is built with kindness, respect, humility and confidence. Hiding, denying or making excuses for a sinful choice only creates instability and contempt.

Prayer: *Lord, You know I'm scared to bare my soul and emotions before my stepkids. I'm afraid they will take advantage of me, and hurt me more than they already have. But I trust You. I want to be like Jesus in every area in my life. And that means admitting when I'm wrong. Give me the words, I trust You with the results. Amen.*

~ Laura

Strength in Weakness

"And He said to me, 'My grace is sufficient for you, for My strength is made perfect in weakness.' Therefore most gladly I will rather boast in my infirmities, that the power of Christ may rest upon me" (2 Corinthians 12:9 NKJV).

Thought for the Day: It takes strength to admit weakness and ask for help.

I grew up in a family where you didn't talk about pain. To share your struggles exposed weakness and that was frowned upon. I went through my adolescent years being told my feelings weren't real. I quickly learned to stuff down my emotions and paint on a happy face each morning. I believed love was conditional and I checked off all the right boxes to achieve it. To the outside world, I had it all together. On the inside, I was crumbling and feared I was weak because I hurt.

When my first husband left me, my heart was shattered and my mind confused. I had done all the things a good wife should do, yet he left. I could no longer pretend all was well and hide behind a false exterior. I was weak. I was broken. I needed my Savior to carry me.

Completely overwhelmed, I admitted my feelings, and on my knees, reached out for help. I discovered a freedom I had never felt before. While the circumstances in my life were devastating, I felt a strength that only comes from Christ.

Now, as a stepmother, I call upon that strength daily. Admitting my weaknesses in my role allows me to connect with others on the journey and to seek godly advice, encouragement and support. When I begin to doubt myself or God's hand in a struggle, I recall that transitional time in my life to remind me that God is always faithful and He does have a plan for me.

Prayer: *Lord, thank you for teaching me that Jesus + nothing = everything. Your grace covers us all and there is no need to fear being weak. It is when I am weakest that I am closest to You. I give You my burdens, and in doing so, draw strength from Your promises knowing You will work it all for my good. I trust in You today and every day. When I need help, remind me I can reach out to You, in vulnerability, finding true strength.*

~ Heather

Creative Solutions

"'For My thoughts are not your thoughts, neither are your ways My ways,' declares the Lord. 'As the heavens are higher than the earth, so are My ways higher than your ways and My thoughts than your thoughts'" (Isaiah 55:8-9 NIV).

Thought for the Day: We find hope when we follow His ways.

Excited about our first vacation as a stepfamily, we headed to the airport before dawn with our four kids — off to the mountains to experience the beauty and euphoria of snow skiing. It didn't take long, however, before tempers began to rise. An unusual snow report cancelled our second flight after countless hours in the airport. While we waited to re-schedule with hundreds of other passengers, my husband, Randy, and I began to argue. As my two young daughters cried and tugged on my pant leg, I walked away from the crowd to pray for our next steps as Randy made decisions. We needed supernatural help.

Randy booked flights for the next day and scheduled a shuttle for a nearby hotel. It wasn't the plan we wanted and grumpy attitudes followed. When we arrived, Randy booked two rooms and suggested my girls and I stay in one, while he and his kids resided next door. Too much togetherness had taken a toll, and our newly-blended family needed time apart. An unusual suggestion, it helped ease the stress for the evening and allowed renewed spirits to start again the next day.

Stepfamily struggles often require creative solutions. They require an open mind in unchartered water as we look to God to direct our way.

God has directed my path through windy roads with question marks, potholes with bruises, and stormy weather with thunderous commands. But I've learned, when I follow His ways, I find hope and victory in the end.

Prayer: *Thank you, Lord, that You promise to help us find our way when we pivot off course. Direct my path as a stepmom and help me remember that I can trust You, even when I don't understand the journey.*

~ Gayla

The Drama: Does it Ever End?

"A hot-tempered man stirs up conflict, but a man slow to anger calms strife" (Proverbs 15:18 HCSB).

Thought for the Day: At all times — be prepared.

After twenty-nine years as a stepmom you would think I've encountered all there is to the journey, wouldn't you?

Nope.

Recently, at a family gathering a situation occurred that shocked me. I thought to myself, "Really, a new type of drama. I thought we were past all of this."

Nope.

I had a decision to make. I could slap the person who was making poor choices, but it's possible my pastor-husband would lose his job over that. (Then how would we pay for my lawyer and the bail? Besides, orange isn't my best color and jumpsuits are a real challenge in the ladies room. In addition, it might be hard to convince others I'm The Smart Stepmom from a prison cell).

Better response: step back, Laura and take time to re-think. So I asked God to help me see the situation through the other person's eyes. And voila... He did!! Suddenly, I understood the hurt. The negative response was due to rejection, and given the same circumstances, I might react the same way.

God showed me how to forgive, and pray for this person. The situation didn't change, but the anger did.

And no handcuffs — a pure bonus!

Prayer: *God, this stepfamily stuff can trigger my anger button faster than anything else. Help me to slow down, and think through my words and choices in the heat of the moment. Show me that it's not always necessary to defend myself. Sometimes, stepping away and keeping silent is the wisest response. You are my defender. You judge with an unbiased heart and mind. I surrender.*

~ Laura

Broken and Blessed

"Trust in the Lord with all your heart, and do not lean on your own understanding. In all your ways acknowledge Him, and He will make straight your paths" (Proverbs 3:5-6 ESV).

Thought for the Day: God doesn't call you to live in your own strength. He walks with you, and on hard days, He carries you.

"I can't do this anymore!" Lying on the bathroom floor, I cried out to God. "I can't keep trying and loving and getting hurt over and over again. It's too hard."

As I lay there in a puddle of my own tears, I heard a gentle whisper. *"You can't, but I can."*

Those simple words spoke to my heart and reminded me it is only through Christ's strength that I endure. Blended family living wasn't what I thought it would be. I had foolishly arrived at the conclusion that I could make our family picture perfect and glue all our broken pieces together. I had been trying to do it in my own strength. That was a big mistake.

I picked myself up and waited to hear what God had to tell me. I had been afraid to hear what God might ask me to do. I wanted the easy life — the life so many other families seemed to have. God was calling me to trust Him. To let Him lead. To live in His strength and take rest in His Word.

Why is it we often say we have faith yet we don't live it? Stepfamily life demands we daily place our faith in God's plan, trusting that all we go through will somehow honor Him. This truth keeps me grounded and gives me strength on my journey. When I find myself starting to say "I can't....", I hear His whisper "but I can."

Prayer: *Lord, I cannot do this without You. Help me to call upon Your strength and rest in Your promises. Whisper to me in those times when I feel like going back in time. When I start to feel hopeless, fill me with Your hope and peace. Make me a model for my family of endurance and a Christ-like heart of joy and grace.*

~ Heather

It's Okay to be Different

"Accept one another, then, just as Christ accepted you, in order to bring praise to God" (Romans 15:7 NIV).

Thought for the Day: It's okay to be different.

I couldn't help but laugh as I read my son's description of our family. I found his elementary schoolwork titled "My Family" while I cleaned out his closet, and the paper caught my attention:

> "We are a family of seven. I have no full blood brothers or sisters. I have a brother named Payton and three sisters named Jamie, Jodi, and Adrianne. Jamie and Jodi have the same mom as me but a different dad. Payton and Adrianne have the same dad as me but a different mom. Jamie and Jodi are stepsisters to Payton and Adrianne. My family is complicated and few people understand us, but it's my family."

Life in a blended family can seem complicated. We look, talk, and act differently than those in traditional families. We might have different last names. And we often try to hide the fact we're a blended family because we know we're different.

However, our family has discovered that, over time, some of that changes. The love among stepsiblings and half siblings and stepparents and stepchildren grows to look and feel similar to those in traditional families. God's healing power transforms relationships. We will always be a blended family, born of loss, but we no longer carry the shame of brokenness.

Prayer: *Dear Father, help me to accept the differentness of our family. Heal our relationships and draw us together by Your power and in Your time.*

~ Gayla

My Big Mouth

"Therefore, since we are surrounded by such a great cloud of witnesses, let us throw off everything that hinders and the sin that so easily entangles, and let us run with perseverance the race marked out for us" (Hebrews 12:1 NIV).

Thought for the Day: Learn your greatest area of weakness, and then ask God to teach you to overcome.

Usually, a follower of Christ has one sin that is a primary area of weakness. It's the "Achilles Heel" or an area of weakness where the devil comes back to attack over and over. For me, my vulnerability is in having a critical, condescending tongue.

Place a naturally fault-finding woman into a stepfamily scenario and explosions aren't far behind. Let's face it; there are a plethora of problem people and juicy flaws to criticize!

An inability to tame my tongue has been a long time battle. I only had one thing going for me. I hated having a critical tongue. I truly wanted to stop. And that's all God needed. I began praying that God would help me to think through the consequences of my words before I said them.

When I see the hurt look on my husband's face after a blast of my wounding words, it forces me to admit that I'm whittling away at my marriage and betraying my vows. If I want our union to survive, it means I must learn how to discipline my tongue. Many times that means "zip the lips."

God helped me to think through my marital goal. "When you breathe your last, Laura, what do you want your home's legacy to be?" That was easy. I want a home at peace and a unified, content marriage. I want to be remembered as a wife and stepmom who brings peace into the midst of conflict, not one who exacerbates the problems.

I finally admitted that the momentary satisfaction of spewing my frustrations at him wasn't achieving my desired goal. This doesn't mean ignoring or denying problems. That is a perversion of peace. But rather addressing the issues in a calm, kind manner.

Taming my tongue is a choice. A very hard choice because I'm often right!! However, being right became less important when I had the opportunity to respond like Christ. Whatever your area of temptation, God knows and He has an answer for victory.

Prayer: *Lord Jesus, help me. My words get me into big trouble and I don't know how to stop. In the moment it feels so good to release my angry thoughts, but afterwards I feel terrible. I know this conviction is from You, Holy Spirit. And I believe You can teach me how to discern when it's wise to speak up and lovingly share my feelings, and when to keep silent. Thank you.*

~ Laura

Don't Drink the Poison

"Do not withhold Your mercy from me, Lord; may Your love and Your truth always protect me" (Psalm 40:11 NASB).

Thought for the Day: You are not defined by the words of another.

I am typically never at a loss for words. Yet on a shopping trip a few weeks ago, I found myself speechless. I was at Target looking at some boots when I overheard a mom talking to her preschool daughter.

The young girl said, "Vicki has these shoes. Maybe Sandy will buy me some."

"Never," replied the mother. "She only buys things for her kids, and you aren't hers. She's your stepmom and she only cares about her kids, not you."

Ouch! Now, I don't know the story behind that family, but I do know the look I saw on the young girl's face—sadness.

Right there I paused to pray for that woman and her child. Prayer is the most powerful protection against dark thoughts.

You cannot control what the mother of your stepchildren tells her kids. While you may live in the pain of what those words do to the children and how they can often alienate them from your home, you cannot control it.

Understand that if others are telling lies about you and/or your husband, that is just a reflection of their insecurities. No one who is secure in themselves has a need or desire to put down another. While it can be very painful to know your stepchild is being poisoned against you, respond in prayer and find peace knowing the hate comes from an unhealed hurt in the one who speaks it.

Prayer: *Dear Heavenly Father, please guard the heart of my stepchildren. Help them to know they are loved. May they turn to You to understand their worth and may they know that they are loved by their father and me. If there is an unhealed hurt in their mother, please bring her to a place where she can make peace with past hurts and live fully in the present. May the children be blessed with parents and stepparents who follow after You.*

~ Heather

How to Find Contentment

"...I have learned to be content whatever the circumstances" (Philippians 4:11 NIV).

Thought for the Day: I can experience contentment, regardless of my situation.

"My stepchildren have unhealed wounds that keep them from bonding with me. I imagine they're telling themselves, 'My mom already left. I'm waiting for you to leave too.'" The words of my friend Jill saddened me. Her stepchildren's mother had chosen a life of alcoholism, creating deep wounds with her children. As a result, Jill had been forced into a full-time stepmom role with challenges she didn't create and couldn't fix.

Determined to break through their walls, Jill changed her career path to work from home, allowing more time to connect with her stepchildren. Without children of her own, she enjoyed the maternal role that came naturally for her. But the bonds she had hoped for didn't happen quickly. It wasn't long before depression set in.

As stepmoms, our challenges often feel overwhelming. With God's help, however, we can learn to be content with our circumstances. We don't have to let the actions of our unhappy stepchild steal our joy or influence our behavior. When we decide we won't give that power over to another person, we find internal peace and joy.

Jill learned to disconnect from the moodiness of her stepchildren and respond with an attitude of forgiveness rather than anger. Unable to change their hurt, she could control her own emotions, which influenced how she reacted toward them. An internal peace flooded her soul as she learned to be content in imperfect surroundings.

Prayer: *Heavenly Father, my home has troubles. Show me how to be content in the midst of sadness. I need Your help. I can't do this alone.*

~ Gayla

The Mother-in-Law

"A gentle answer deflects anger, but harsh words make tempers flare" (Proverbs 15:1 NLT).

Thought for the Day: God will help me to be kind to all people, even those who hurt me.

When my brother became a full-time single parent to two little girls, aged two and six, my mom and I stepped in to help him. I sincerely love my nieces as if they were my own kids. And I enjoyed every minute that I was able to be a "surrogate mom" to them.

When he remarried, I had a hard time letting go. I truly embraced my new sister-in-law and her two children, plus I felt she was a great mate for him. However, I wasn't sure she would love the girls and care for them as I did. My nieces had already suffered so much loss and pain. I wanted to protect them.

That was foolish.

My brother and his newly formed stepfamily needed time to bond. My sister-in-law needed time to learn how to be a smart stepmom. She didn't need a meddling sister-in-law.

You may be dealing with in-laws who are hurt, afraid or resentful about the remarriage. Learning how to respond and communicate with loving reassurance that you desire for the in-laws to maintain a great relationship with the kids can turn a tumultuous situation around toward harmony.

Prayer: *Jesus, my husband's family hurts me and they don't like me. I think they wish he had never married me. I can't control their feelings or attitudes, but I can control how I respond to them. Your Word tells me there is a way to react that builds a bridge of harmony, rather than detachment. Show me how, Lord. Your servant is listening.*

~ Laura

Not a Mind-Reader

"Rather, speaking the truth in love, we are to grow up in every way into him who is the head, into Christ" (Ephesians 4:15 ESV).

Thought for the Day: God keeps us in step with one another when we step through our day with Him.

My husband loves me. That means he should understand me and know what I like and want, right? Wrong. My husband does love me, but he's not a mind-reader. When I expect him to know what I need in our relationship, I set myself up for disappointment.

If I want my husband to know something I need to speak it in truth and love. Sometimes that means giving him a hint for my birthday. Other times it means prefacing a conversation about his kids. If I want my husband to just listen to my heart and not move into problem-solving mode, I need to tell him that. "I want to share some hard stuff that happened and I'd just like you to listen," is a healthy way to ask for what I want.

God is the only one who can read my mind and my heart. Most days, I'm not sure I even want Him to. Yet I desire my husband to understand my thoughts.

Expecting your spouse to anticipate and give you what you want without ever communicating it is a recipe for unmet expectations and frustration. Recognize what you would like from your husband and then ask him for it. Speaking the truth in love doesn't guarantee you will get what you ask for, but it does diminish disappointment from unmet expectations.

Prayer: *Dear Heavenly Father, help me to recognize what I want from my husband and to communicate it in a godly way. Prepare my heart to speak and prepare my husband to listen. May our communication with each other be a blessing to You and to our marriage. Help us to speak to one another with kindness, compassion and truth.*

~ Heather

Learning to Trust

"'For I know the plans I have for you,' declares the Lord, 'plans to prosper you and not to harm you, plans to give you hope and a future'" (Jeremiah 29:11 NIV).

Thought for the Day: God's ways are sovereign. We may not understand His plan but we can trust His heart.

"I just got the news. She passed away earlier today." My stepchildren's mother had been ill but the finality of my husband's words saddened me. My heart ached as I thought about my teenage stepdaughter and stepson facing life without their beloved mom. Rippling effects from the tragedy would soon seep into our home.

It's easy to trust God when life marches on without hardship. But when we face circumstances we don't understand and can't change, faith wavers. My husband and I had prayed God would heal his ex-wife. But God had a different plan.

Questions without answers overwhelmed me. Would the children move across state lines and come live with us? Could our home accommodate two more? How would they cope as they struggled to accept their mom was gone? What could we do to help with their troubled emotions? I knew I had to trust God with what lay ahead.

Answers didn't come quickly. Tension mounted as we waded through months of confusion and anxiety. My husband and I didn't see eye to eye on solutions. When we finally surrendered to God's plan, although different than what we desired, peace engulfed us.

My stepdaughter began college shortly following her mom's death without relocating. My stepson remained another year with his stepdad and younger half-brother before coming to our home to complete high school. Healing began when we gave up control of the circumstances and trusted God with the outcome.

Prayer: *Dear Lord, thank you for Your unending provision, even during difficult days. Help me to trust You with my circumstances.*

~ Gayla

When Wrong Seems Right

"I tell you, her many sins are forgiven because she loves much. But the one who has been forgiven little, loves little" (Luke 7:47 NLV).

Thought for the Day: "Preach the Gospel at all times; when necessary use words." Francis of Assisi

A common cry from the Christian stepmom is what to do when she and her husband seek to have a God-honoring family, but the kids witness the opposite in the other home.

The answer: Accept that you cannot change what goes on in the mom's home, and then use the situation to impart heavenly wisdom. Notice I didn't suggest using it to bash, judge, Bible thump or criticize the mom. Having a "What Would Jesus Do" response will require a significant amount of prayer and a Holy Spirit filled, Christ-like attitude.

It's easy to condemn the mom, and point a finger at her sinfulness. This will clearly communicate to her children that dad and stepmom are self-righteous, sanctimonious and out-of-touch prudes.

Jesus encountered sinful women all the time. There is a way to address sin without attacking the sinner. The problem is that we Christians aren't very good at it. We default to the easier method of throwing stones.

How did Jesus respond to a sinner? He spoke the truth in love, a difficult task for us mere mortals. This is why we must seek divine guidance from the Heavenly Papa.

God is very good at humbling me. When I start to look down my nose at another person He takes me down "memory lane" and reveals what I was, and would be, without Him. I'd be following the same sinful, crooked, destructive path as others if I hadn't surrendered to His salvation and forgiveness.

Prayer: *Holy God, forgive me. I am a woman who sins. I judge. I condemn. I criticize. Even if I don't do these things with my tongue, I do them with my mind and actions. Heal me from the sin of pride. Make me like you, Jesus. Please make me like you.*

~ Laura

Stepmom Blessing

"And the God of peace himself sanctify you wholly; and may your spirit and soul and body be preserved entire, without blame at the coming of our Lord Jesus Christ. Faithful is he that calleth you, who will also do it" (1 Thessalonians 5:23-24 ASV).

Thought for the Day: If God has called you to be the heart of your blended family, He will equip you to live it.

The phrase, "They are so much better off with you in their lives," is something I hear regularly. Really? I don't think my stepdaughters have gotten the memo.

Realistically, it would have been best for my stepkids if their mom and dad had maintained a strong marriage and never divorced. They would be growing up minus stepfamily complications and the word "step" would only apply to their front porch and to things they need to accomplish to reach a goal, not to people in their lives.

Yet, here we are, in a big, blended family of eight. Our steplife is messy and complicated with both love and pain sprinkled in. As a full-time stepmom, I balance honoring my stepdaughters' mother with being a mom to them. While my stepdaughters benefit from my physical presence, emotionally I am a constant reminder that their mom is gone. That causes them to push me away at times.

As stepmom, it is the role you play, not you personally, that a stepchild lashes out against. You are a reminder that their mom and dad will not be together, and that can be very hard on a child of any age. I encourage you to stand firm in the knowledge that you are where God wants you to be and rest in His love for you.

Prayer: *Dear Heavenly Father, I am grateful to be a wife and mother, yet I struggle with many of the duties attached. Help me to work through my hurts and to live in Your truths. I know when my stepchildren are hardest to be around, that is when they need me most. I desire to give them consistent direction and love, and to model a Christ-like attitude. Help me, Lord, as I seek to help my family.*

~ Heather

Let God Direct Your Path

"Trust in the Lord with all your heart, and lean not on your own understanding; In all your ways acknowledge Him, And He shall direct your paths" (Proverbs 3:5-6 NKJV).

Thought for the Day: God wants to direct our paths.

I had convinced myself I couldn't pass the graduate statistics class in my master's program. I lacked only two classes to finish my coursework, but I began to question why I had even started. Doubt consumed every thought.

Finally, I sought counsel from the professor. Happy to help, he patiently explained what I didn't understand. He didn't degrade my lack of understanding or question my ability to pass his course. He simply put me on a different path.

Similarly, I often questioned my capability as a young stepmom. Doubt consumed every fiber as I convinced myself I would fail. Finally, I sought God's help for direction and encouragement.

A few weeks later, I learned of a stepcouple support class about to begin at a local church. Camaraderie with others on the same journey and a Bible-based study for stepfamilies gave me the courage I needed to keep going. Encouragement from other couples and better understanding of stepfamily dynamics gave me compassion for my stepchildren and wisdom in my responses to those around me.

Prayer: *Dear Lord, I don't have all the answers to my stepfamily struggles. But I know You do. Direct my path to Your solutions and give me courage to keep going when I want to quit.*

~ Gayla

Victorious Living

"God has removed my disgrace" (Genesis 30:23 NLT).

Thought for the Day: With God's help, I can have victory over anything destructive.

Since my childhood, shame has plagued a large portion of my life. As an adult I didn't know where it came from or how it had manifested itself so deeply into my soul. But disgrace hovered, imprisoned and devoured much of my thought life.

With the aid of professional help, I discovered that I had saddled myself with the lie that I was to blame for my parent's divorce. As an eight year old, I took on the responsibility and the humiliation of being solely responsible for the demise of my family. That's a heavy oppression for a little girl's mind.

Then the stepmom journey reignited the old flame of shame. There were days when the stress of stepfamily living prompted wicked thoughts such as, "You call yourself a Christian! How could a godly woman have such horrible thoughts—and toward children no less? You should be ashamed of yourself."

And I wept—believing the lie that I was a horrible stepmom.

It wasn't until I discovered that other stepmoms had similar feelings. That's when I realized it was normal to wrestle with thoughts of wishing I could go back to the simpler life. Laura isn't wicked. I merely had to learn how to tame and tromp on those "stepmonster moments" that attempt to heap shame, fear and self-loathing upon stepfamilies.

Once I asked Jesus to help me have freedom from the burden of that implanted toxic childhood shame, I began learning how to walk in victory.

Is shame dictating your thoughts? Even if the humiliation you carry is due to poor choices, today is the day to find freedom. God is willing to heal you.

Prayer: *Dear Lord, I want freedom. I want the mind of Christ filled with truth, peace, and assurance. You are the only One who heals our shame. Teach me how to triumph over destructive thoughts.*

~ Laura

Fresh Canvas

"For freedom Christ has set us free; stand firm therefore, and do not submit again to a yoke of slavery" (Galatians 5:1 ESV).

Thought for the Day: Dwell on God's Word when others want to dwell on your past mistakes.

When we come to God with our transgressions, He is mighty to offer grace and mercy. If God forgives us, no man or woman can hold something over us.

We spend so much time trying to prove we are worthy when God already knows and believes that we are. Letting go of the need for approval from others is the most freeing experience. When we truly let go of what others think of us, we can embrace the gift of love and mercy God so freely gives.

We are all human, and therefore, we all make mistakes. Nothing we do or say is beyond God's forgiveness, mercy and grace. Take a minute to soak that in. God gives us the gift of a fresh start each day and we have the responsibility to live in His truths.

God does not chain you to your past. Don't let someone else do that to you. You are impacted by your yesterdays, yet you are not defined by them. You live today smarter from your past mistakes, but you must live fully in the present. You can do it. I believe in you!

Prayer: *Dear Heavenly Father, thank you for the gift of a fresh start. I have said and done things that are not of You yet You love me anyway. I cannot comprehend the gift of Your mercy and grace. Just as I welcome it, help me to give it to others around me. When I am feeling chained to past mistakes, help me to remember You have set me free. Allow me to live smarter from my mistakes and to focus on my today and tomorrow.*

~ Heather

Changing Residence

"Jesus Christ is the same yesterday, today, and forever" (Hebrews 13:8 NLT).

Thought for the Day: Although our circumstances change, Jesus Christ remains the same.

When a stepchild wants to change residences, it's natural to begin soul searching. But, the reality is, it probably has nothing to do with you and everything to do with your stepchild.

When my stepdaughter moved to her mom's house as an adolescent, I naturally assumed responsibility for it. If I'd been a better stepmom, perhaps she'd have stayed. I soon realized, however, that she wanted the bond and influence of her mother during her teenage years.

It's not unusual for stepchildren who yearn for a deeper relationship with their other parent to consider a move. As they seek to find identity, they look to their other parent for the missing link. Conflicted emotions and the tug of loyalty ties also contribute to a desire to try out the other home, particularly during their teen years. Open, honest conversations, that don't inflict guilt or anger, can help your stepchild explore his or her options. If a move does happen, however, don't assume it's your fault.

My husband and I leaned into the Lord as we endured a difficult transition. His unchanging presence and unending comfort gave us strength for our changing circumstances that year, and many more that followed.

Prayer: *Thank you, dear Lord, for Your promise that You never change. I cling to You for comfort during times of unwanted change. I can't do this without You. Please walk beside me and show me Your presence.*

~ Gayla

Look Up!

"... because we know that suffering produces perseverance; perseverance, character; and character, hope. And hope does not put us to shame, because God's love has been poured out into our hearts through the Holy Spirit, Who has been given to us." (Romans 5: 3b-5 NIV).

Thought for the Day: Even on the darkest days, we have a hope that never dims.

As a stepmom I've had some dark days, times when help and hope were hard to find. Where does a woman turn, when life feels bleak and having a happy family seems impossible?

A smart stepmom does what King David did when he was being hunted like an animal. She shifts her eyes off the circumstances and onto the Holy One. David affirms his source of strength, "But You, O Lord, are a shield about me, My glory, and the One who lifts my head. I was crying to the Lord with my voice, And He answered me from His holy mountain" (Psalm 3:3-4 NASV).

David's circumstances didn't change, his son still sought to kill him. Your stepfamily might not change either. The question is where will you focus? Will you allow the sorrow of today to transform you into a woman of tomorrow who fixes her eyes on Jesus? Will you permit the Holy Spirit to use this uninvited suffering to produce a hope and confidence that overcomes any hardship? Will you choose to have confidence in the One who never fails or leaves us?

This day I encourage you to let God lift your head, the same way He did for King David.

Look up.

Prayer: *Almighty God, I don't know what tomorrow holds, but I know the One who holds it. I am your precious daughter and I am loved. The things and relationships on earth will pass, therefore, I will keep my eyes on a higher prize. Many faithful people suffer hardships; it's not unique to me. I choose to allow this situation to strengthen my faith. Transform my mind, Holy Spirit. I'm Yours. Amen.*

~ Laura

Letting Go of the Need to Know

"I can do all things through Christ who strengthens me" (Philippians 4:13 NKJV).

Thought for the Day: Reasons are personal and I don't need to know the "why" of everything that happens around me.

As stepmoms, we live in many states. The state of confusion and frustration. The state of joy and happiness. The state of isolation and rejection. The state of anger and bitterness. Okay, so you get the picture.

I find that I used to spend a lot of time in the state of WHY? Getting there was so easy. WHY would my stepdaughter lie to her dad? WHY would the ex-wife say horrible things about me? WHY wouldn't my stepdaughters' mom call them on holidays? And WHY would she send them photos of her "new" family? WHY? WHY? WHY?

I have learned something very important about living in the state of WHY— you end up in the land of Misery. Often there are no answers to the WHY's, and even when there are, the likelihood they will be appeasing is slim to none.

Through prayer, we stepmoms can usually discern when we truly need to know WHY. My advice to you, dear friends, is to live in the state of self-care. Live in the state of not taking things personally. Live in the state of joy in your heart and peace in your home.

Hold onto Jesus and not to questions that may have no answers.

Prayer: *Lord, help me to discern when knowing why something happened is necessary and when I should let it go. Then help me to do it. I often want to hold onto things I want to understand, but they just weigh me down. In those times, help me to hold on to You instead. Fill me with peace and remove my need to know why.*

~ Heather

The Danger of Denial

"Be alert and of sober mind. Your enemy the devil prowls around like a roaring lion looking for someone to devour" (I Peter 5:8 NIV).

Thought for the Day: We experience victory in our homes when we face our challenges head-on, looking to God for direction.

I didn't want to accept the truth. I had convinced myself that my 6-year-old daughter's erratic behavior was normal for a child of divorce. Add to that, remarriage with a stepdad and stepsiblings moving into her home. As her emotional outbursts became more frequent, however, I had to accept she needed professional help.

Satan wants to destroy our homes. He wins if he can camouflage our problems so we don't see them or recognize their danger. But if we stay alert and ready to take action when we sense God's call of urgency, we experience victory.

It seemed easier to live in denial than admit my daughter wasn't coping well. But I soon learned that wearing a blindfold to an escalating issue in our home created tension for everyone. I needed to take the first step to help her find healing.

Now, a thriving young adult, my daughter lives a life committed to the Lord in full-time ministry. She finds joy in helping young girls reach beyond their struggles and find healing in the Lord. It all started when I walked out of denial.

Prayer: *Heavenly Father, please take the blindfold off my eyes to areas in my home that need help. Give me the courage to take the first step toward healing.*

~ Gayla

Am I Lovable?

"Others were given in exchange for you. I traded their lives for yours because you are precious to me. You are honored, and I love you" (Isaiah 43: 4 NLT).

Thought for the Day: I am lovable because God says so. Even when people reject me, God says I'm beautiful.

For forty years the prophet Jeremiah remained faithful and obedient to God even though no one liked, appreciated, or listened to him. Even his family and friends rejected him. He was banished.

Life as a stepmom can feel like that. Lonely. Isolated. Evicted. Dismissed.

That's when it's time to view ourselves through a different lens. God longs for us to know we aren't discarded or alone.

It's a promise. He never leaves. He never changes. He never abandons.

When the kids, stepkids, husband, ex-wife, or mother-in-law throws an emotional punch with hurtful words or rejection, it's time to get very quiet and listen to the One who knows you best. Listen to the One who knows your soul — your true heart.

He whispers, "What is the truth? I'm not asking how you feel right now; I'm asking you to ponder truth. The fact is I love you. You are precious. Stop listening to the lethal lies that claim you are unlovable, ungodly, unhealthy and undesirable. Instead, listen to my heartbeat. It beats for you, beloved one! I gave my life for you because you are worth saving!"

If no one has ever revealed that God views you as His enchanting, delightful, and honorable daughter — let me be the first.

It's true. Just ask Him.

Prayer: *Lord, it's hard for me to view myself as wonderful when the people all around me say the opposite. It hurts to feel so rejected and alone. Please bring other stepmoms into my path so that we can encourage and remind each other that we are not alone.*

~ Laura

God's Exchange Program

"My flesh and my heart may fail, but God is the strength of my heart and my portion forever" (Psalm 73:26 NIV).

Thought for the Day: Exchange your hurts for His hope.

It's true. The job of a stepmom is tough. You are called upon to do things that do not come naturally to you. If you try to do this job in your own power, you will end up exhausted, angry, and bitter. Doing it with a spirit-filled strength won't make your struggles disappear, but it will enable you to be a stepparent with more joy and peace than you could have experienced on your own.

"When I married my husband, I didn't realize I was marrying his ex-wife and all her drama," one stepmom shared with me. How true. A stepmom never truly knows what she is getting into despite the often unwelcome warnings from well-meaning friends. She may not realize in addition to marrying her husband, she is getting his ex-wife or deceased wife, and their kids, as well as in-laws and former in-laws. Not only does she "inherit " these relationships, but she gains all the trials that come with each one.

Navigating the family forest of steprelationships can be exhausting. Thankfully, with God we don't have to go at this alone. He knows the people in our lives. He knows their hearts and their hurts. He knows this task is hard. He knows we are going to make mistakes.

Embrace what's hard and give it to Him. Exchange your hurts for His hope.

Prayer: *Thank you, God, that You don't call me to be perfect. You only ask that I walk in obedience to Your words. Your expectations for my performance are much more realistic than mine. Help me to let go of the need to control the things that hurt me and to instead seek Your peace. I believe You have me right where You want me to be. I will exchange my struggles for Your comfort, hope, and peace. On days when I don't know how I'll get through, I will strive to rest in You.*

~ Heather

The Power of Boundaries

"And the Lord God commanded the man, 'You are free to eat from any tree in the garden; but you must not eat from the tree of the knowledge of good and evil, for when you eat from it you will certainly die'" (Genesis 2:16-17 NIV).

Thought for the Day: Thriving relationships require healthy boundary setting.

As a family of six, our house was full of shoes! I remember the conversation clearly. "If everyone leaves three pairs of shoes by the door, we'll have 18 pairs of shoes here." Seeking to teach my stepson that shoes belong in the bedroom, I gave a simple illustration and concluded with, "If I have to pick up your shoes again I'll put them in the attic where they'll stay for a week."

I wasn't a popular stepmom that day. However, when I maintained some sense of order in our home, everything ran smoother. If I communicated my standard with a consequence, my stepson understood its importance. One pair of shoes went to the attic before the boundary was taken seriously.

As stepmoms, we teach others how to treat us through our actions, inactions, communication or silence. If we allow our stepchildren to constantly trample over our requests, we set ourselves up for an embittered relationship and create self-centered adults in the process.

God gives us the perfect example of boundaries in the Garden of Eden with consequences for disobedience—a pattern worth following.

Prayer: *Dear Lord, thank you for Your example in the Garden of Eden. Please give me wisdom and courage to maintain healthy boundaries in our home.*

~ Gayla

Moving From Panic to Peace

"Call to Me and I will answer you and tell you great and incomprehensible things you do not know" (Jeremiah 33:3 HCSB).

Thought for the Day: I cannot control the choices of others. I can control how I respond to the choices of others.

Have you ever found yourself in a stepmom situation where you truly didn't know what to do? A circumstance where there doesn't seem to be right direction? I have.

It might be a pending court date, a financial upheaval, a stepchild who is telling lies, a spouse who accuses you of not loving his kids, or an ex-wife that is determined to destroy your marriage.

That is when it's crucial to remember that God knows, understands, and sees things that we cannot. He sees into the heavenly realm. He has answers when all seems impossible.

What a relief it was to discover that I don't need to have all the answers, I merely need to lean on the One who does. But how does a control freak like me do that? It's often necessary to get alone in a quiet place where the taunting voices of bewilderment can be stifled. It can be as simple as taking a fifteen minute walk out in God's creation.

During the down times, compile a list of scriptures that remind you that there is no circumstance bigger than God, and that He is in your corner!! Two of my favorite resources are: *Praying God's Word*, by Beth Moore, and A Daily Prayer For Freedom by John Eldredge from his book *Waking the Dead*.

When a crisis hits, having verses handy to read OUT LOUD if necessary is how to capture perplexing thoughts before they transform into panic mode.

Prayer: *Lord, I admit that stepfamily living has cornered me into situations where I'm confused and easily stressed out. I desire to seek You for clarity and confirmation regarding what is the right thing to do. Help me not to lean on my own understanding, because emotions can distort the truth. Instead guide me toward perfect wisdom from the Bible, godly friends, and Your divine intervention.*

~ Laura

Hitting the Pause Button

"Be still, and know that I am God. I will be exalted among the nations, I will be exalted in the earth!" (Psalm 46:10 ESV).

Thought for the Day: Being still in God's presence won't solve your problems but it will bring you peace.

It is natural for me to allow myself to become anxious, especially when it comes to my blended family. If I don't catch myself, I can start running down a dead-end road in my head.

When I am still, I can hear God. And when I hear Him, I feel peace.

Early in our marriage, my husband and I had very different responses to a behavior we didn't like in one of the kids. I was sure my way was right and my husband was sure he was the one with the correct formula. We had both believed we had been successful as single parents and we weren't used to sharing decision-making. Through much trial and error and time in prayer, I have come to realize choosing one way or the other doesn't dictate a quick fix to a stepchild issue. Yet being still in God's Word does make an immediate difference.

When I quiet my mind and dwell only on God's words I feel the peace that comes with trusting Him and His word instead of thrusting forth with my will.

There is no perfect way to raise children, yet debate about it between a stepmother and her husband can cause great strife. I have learned that God will direct my steps, but I must be still enough to listen to His words.

Prayer: *Dear Lord, please help me quiet my spirit, pause and be still. You promise to give me peace and hope and to direct my steps. May I allow You to do just that. Pausing to pray and let You fill me is my heart's desire. In those moments when I want to run in my own direction, help me to see that the roadblocks You put up are to force me to be still, to listen to You, and to trust in Your plans. I know they are for my good.*

~ Heather

Stinkin' Thinkin'

"Finally brothers, whatever is true, whatever is honorable, whatever is just, whatever is pure, whatever is lovely, whatever is commendable — if there is any moral excellence and if there is any praise — dwell on these things" (Philippians 4:8 HCSB).

Thought for the Day: I choose to focus on positive thoughts about my stepfamily.

I'm guilty of stinkin' thinkin' sometimes. How about you? Do you know what it looks like? Here are some examples:

- My stepson will never like me so why do I bother trying to have a relationship with him?
- No one understands my feelings of rejection as a stepmom; I'm living on an island by myself.
- My husband has no idea how difficult this is. It's useless to talk to him.
- Re-marriage is just too hard. Looks like I'm headed for divorce again.

It's dangerous when I get tangled in a web of negative thinking. Stinkin' thinkin' creates a bitter quitter. But some days, in the midst of conflict or misunderstanding, my mind heads down the wrong road. I have to be intentional to think positively, but I've noticed what a difference it makes in my stepfamily relationships.

Prayer: *Dear Father, please help me stay positive on hard days. Help me to think honorable, lovely, and commendable thoughts about my stepchildren. Guide my thoughts when they start to go astray.*

~ Gayla

Ambushed!

"I press on toward the goal to win the prize for which God has called me heavenward in Christ Jesus" (Philippians 3:14 NIV).

Thought for the Day: You didn't know—what you didn't know. It's normal to be surprised by stepfamily complexities.

"There are a number of things I didn't realize," Sherrie, a stepmom of four months shared. "My husband and I thought we were prepared to handle a blended family, but each day we encounter issues we didn't take into consideration."

Sherrie's situation isn't abnormal. When I got married to a man with children I was astonished by the uncertainty of stepfamily living.

Over time, and after seeking numerous resources, I realized my feelings, emotions, and situations weren't unique. Many stepmoms have to overcome issues they didn't expect. With God's grace, time, and a deep desire to learn I made progress.

Don't lose heart. Don't give up.

Sometimes just knowing something is normal is what God uses to encourage us to press on. When we keep our, "eyes on the prize," our focus often shifts from the issues we face to the bigger picture.

One fabulous way to heal from the unexpected situations associated with stepfamily living is to join a stepmom support group or attend a stepmom weekend retreat. In these relaxed, fun settings with other stepmoms you'll learn that the issues you face are normal. And we provide practical tips to help with the journey. For more information www.SisterhoodofStepmoms.com.

Prayer: *Lord, I'm overwhelmed. And if I'm being honest, I'm resentful. I wasn't prepared for the issues I'm now facing. I lay down all these negative emotions before You. Help me to remember that You alone are my strength. Encountering stepfamily situations is normal, and You will hold me up and provide sister stepmoms for support along the way.*

~ Laura

Perspective is Personal

"Be my rock of refuge, to which I can always go; give the command to save me, for you are my rock and my fortress" (Psalm 71:3 NIV).

Thought for the Day: Standing on the Word of God is the only place I want to plant my two feet.

Out to dinner one evening, we couldn't help but overhear the conversation at the table next to us. A woman was ranting to her friend about her ex-husband's new wife. "She gets to be the fun parent," she stated. "She gets to just hang out with my kids. Stepmoms have all the fun."

As I nearly choked on a bite of salad, I had to fight back the need to pull *The Smart Stepmom* out of my purse and stick it in her hand. Surely the yellow highlighted paragraphs and notes in the margins would awaken this woman to the fact that "fun" is the last word a stepmom would use to define her role.

Perspective is not truth. It's simply how someone views another person's life, and it comes through their particular lens. The only perspective that is unchanging is God's.

You can't make your stepkids see your heart. You can't make their mother accept you and encourage her children's relationship with you. You can't control how your husband views you and your relationship with his kids. You can, however, trust and believe in how God sees you and your heart.

God knows your pain and your purpose. He sees what you do and how you navigate a very challenging role.

When untrue things are said about you, go back to the truth—God's truth. Find rest in God's vision of you and His promises to bring you hope and peace.

Prayer: *Dear Heavenly Father, I try so hard to be a good person. It hurts to be told I'm something I am not by people who don't even know me. Help me to rest in Your view of me. You know my heart and You love me. Help me to love myself the way You love me and to see myself through Your eyes. I pray that I can let go of caring what others think of me and find peace in Your love.*

~ Heather

Don't Compare!

"Do not conform to the pattern of this world, but be transformed by the renewing of your mind. Then you will be able to test and approve what God's will is – His good, pleasing and perfect will" (Romans 12:2 NIV).

Thought for the Day: I find contentment when I quit comparing myself to others and turn my mind toward Christ.

My girls call my husband Dad and look to him as their primary father figure. I know from their actions they love him more than words can describe.

I don't doubt my stepchildren's love for me, but I know they will never call me Mom. Loyalty binds create confusing emotions for them.

My ex-husband walked out of my girls' lives for several years when they were young. His lack of presence and influence allowed my girls a stronger relationship with my husband without concern for the feelings of their biological dad. The dynamics with my stepchildren were completely different.

When we compare ourselves or our stepfamilies to relationships in other homes, or even our own home, we create negative images of ourselves. But when we trust God with the path we're on and keep our thoughts focused on Him, we move forward in a positive light.

Prayer: *Heavenly Father, help me erase the negative thoughts that permeate my mind. I don't want to compare myself to others but sometimes it happens so easily. Transform my mind to the mind of Christ. I put my trust in You.*

~ Gayla

Where's the Peace?

"Peace I leave with you, My peace I give to you; not as the world gives do I give to you" (John 14:27 NKJV).

Thought for the Day: If I'm willing, I can learn how to think like Christ.

My stepmom journey has included a lot of stress and confusion. Often I couldn't find a way to merely relax. Then, profound teacher, Oswald Chambers, helped me recognize what was wrong. "Whenever peace does not come, wait until it does, or seek to find out why it is not coming... The spirit of simplicity, clarity, and unity is born through the Holy Spirit, not through your decisions."[4]

Chambers isn't claiming we won't face tumultuous times. In essence he is probing into our souls asking, "Where do you run when the waves get high? Are you leaning on your own strength? Is disobedience to God, or self-willed decisions, the cause of conflict?" He pushes me to examine the root reason for my tension, beyond the circumstances.

When I allow the Holy Spirit to reveal deeper reasons, I discover a way to place the issue where it belongs — at the foot of the cross. If I'm in the wrong, it's time to make it right. If others are making poor choices that flow into my home, I learn how to properly address and/or accept what I can't change. If I'm enabling the problem to continue, I learn to set a healthy boundary.

The key is to let God reveal the true reason(s) that reside in my heart. It might be fear, frustration, or an unmet desire. It could be that I'm attempting to force a person (including my spouse) to meet a God-sized need that they can never fill.

The question is, "Will I let the Holy Spirit teach me how to look and live above, below, and around the circumstance? Or will I let the situation stab me in the heart and punch me in the gut indefinitely?"

God promises to bring peace in the midst of the most traumatic situations. However, we must let go — and look up.

---

[4] Oswald Chambers Publications Assoc. Ltd, *My Utmost for His Highest*, Thomas Nelson Publishers, December 14th, 1935, 1963, 1992

Prayer: *Holy One, You are the Prince of Peace. The Bible says I'm Your child, and that You won't hold back from me anything good. Today, I'm asking. Give me the peace that can only come from resting in You."*

~ Laura

Love Hurts

"The LORD will surely comfort Zion and will look with compassion on all her ruins; he will make her deserts like Eden, her wastelands like the garden of the LORD. Joy and gladness will be found in her, thanksgiving and the sound of singing" (Isaiah 51:3 NIV).

Thought for the Day: Love hurts. God heals.

Last night I watched the movie, *Good Will Hunting*. I am always moved by the scene when Robin William's character is talking to Will (Matt Damon) about pain and loss. He explains, "You can only feel pain when you love another more than you love yourself."

Pondering those words, I wonder if that is the reason it hurts so much when my husband lets me down or when my stepkids reject me. As women, we have a heart to nurture and love others and it can be very painful when we don't feel that love returned. Take solace in the fact that your deep love is the source of the pain you feel.

If you didn't love, it wouldn't hurt so much. Loving in a stepfamily is going to hurt, but we can give that pain to God. He will replace it with peace and hope. God knows your pain before you even call out to Him.

While struggles in my stepfamily hurt, the emotional pain I feel is never stronger than the love I feel when I soak my mind in God's truth. He fills me with a peace that transcends my struggles, and He will fill you with His comfort, too.

Prayer: *Dear Lord, some days I feel so wounded I allow the pain to fill my soul and weigh me down. Please take that pain and replace it with Your hope and love. I understand that it is my love for my family that causes me to hurt so deeply. Oh, how Your heart must ache when I wander from Your path. Yet You always welcome me back with mercy and grace. Help me to model a Christ-like love for those in my family.*

~ Heather

Our Evolving Role

"There is a time for everything, and a season for every activity under heavens" (Ecclesiastes 3:1 NIV).

Thought for the Day: The stepmom role is ever-changing.

I walked to the bus stop in the pouring rain, umbrella in hand, certain my adolescent son would appreciate my gesture of love. I waited patiently until he exited the bus. Then I saw his face, embarrassed. "Mo-o-m! Why did you walk over here? I don't mind the rain."

Suddenly I realized my error. His junior high friends saw his mom waiting for him, wanting to protect him from the rain. That's not cool. He was too old for that. Thankfully, he quickly let it go and began telling me about his day.

Roles change with time. The same holds true for stepmoms. Our role might evolve from one of friendly acquaintance to maternal significance. But—it might not. It could take a step forward and then two steps backward. It might leap to a strong, loving role when your stepchildren leave the home.

There are no guarantees, but if you want to play a significant role, it's important you follow your stepchildren's lead. If they flinch every time you hug them, hold back. If they resist you in a disciplinarian role because you haven't earned their trust, let your spouse take the reins. If they freely offer love, give it in return.

We damage our steprelationships when we try to muscle our way in. God gives us the patience we need for our evolving role, if we ask.

Prayer: *Give me patience and understanding, Lord, in my role as a stepmom. Show me how to love as You love. Remind me that Your timing is always best.*

~ Gayla

No Longer Alone

"As it is, there are many parts, but one body" (1 Corinthians 12:20 NIV).

Thought for the Day:

Turn your eyes upon Jesus,
Look full in His wonderful face,
And the things of earth will grow strangely dim,
In the light of His glory and grace. -Helen H. Lemmel, 1922

Did you know that stepmoms all over the world struggle with the same issues? It's true.

"I live in Australia and I recently downloaded your book for stepmoms. I finally feel so much better knowing that what I feel is normal. It can be very lonely in step mum world! I wanted to thank you for your wisdom, education and validation. It reaches far and wide."- Nicole

There is something that comforts us when we realize, "I am not alone." And for the stepmom you can add, "Look at that. I'm not crazy or wicked after all."

This is one key reason why God created us for community. He knows that too much seclusion is dangerous and He wants us to need each other.

Even though social media has attempted to be a substitute for human contact, it can never meet our need for true connections and companionship. The reason is simple. We were not designed to do life alone.

Isolation is where fear, anger, resentment, shame, retaliation and thoughts of divorce go to breed and multiply. Connecting with stepmoms who have a sincere desire to learn, grow, heal and have fun is essential. Avoid groups that focus on negativity such as: ex-wife bashing, commiserating, and whining.

If there isn't a group near you — maybe God's calling you to start one.

Prayer: *Lord, I'm lonely. Help me to find a healthy community where I can grow as a stepmom. I was created for community, and I desire emotionally healthy friends. Supply them, please.*

~ Laura

What Does Love Look Like?

"My command is this: Love each other as I have loved you" (John 15:12 NIV).

Thought for the Day: I will seek to love others with a Christ-like love.

Loving each other as Christ loves us is a tall order in a stepfamily. It can be really hard to love someone when you don't even like them. Stepmoms ask, " How do I love my stepchildren when they say mean things about me, treat me poorly, or worse, treat their dad and/or my children poorly?"

The Bible depicts many unlovable people—those who cheated, killed, lied and more. One thing they had in common—God loved them.

I have to remember that when someone is the most difficult to be around, that is when they need love and grace the most. God calls me to love all people, not just those who are easy to love.

Once I learned to separate the person from their behavior, it became much easier for me to show love. I recognized their pain caused them to say and do things they normally wouldn't do. I put boundaries up to address their hurtful words and/or actions and prayed for God to keep my heart soft so I could still be loving toward them as a person.

Prayer: *Lord, give me a heart to love each person in my family the way You do. Help my love not be based on their actions, but on my commitment to follow Jesus. I know loving someone doesn't mean condoning their behavior. Help me to create and enforce boundaries where appropriate and to give grace when needed.*

~ Heather

Marital Sacrifices

"And one standing alone can be attacked and defeated, but two can stand back-to-back and conquer; three is even better, for a triple-braided cord is not easily broken" (Ecclesiastes 4:12 TLB).

Thought for the Day: Marriage requires sacrifice.

My dad's words brought tears to my eyes. "Your mom has made a lot of sacrifices for me over the years. It's my turn to make sacrifices for her." As a stoic college professor for decades, my dad never expressed much emotion or appreciation.

I now realize Mom's sacrifices through more than 60 years of marriage didn't go unnoticed. I'm humbled to peer into my parent's lives and watch Dad perform the arduous task of primary caregiver for Mom as the cruel disease of dementia progresses.

Marriage requires sacrifice. I found this to be especially true in the early days of my stepmom role. Sometimes, those sacrifices felt overwhelming. I gave daily to meet the needs of my stepchildren, but reaped few rewards. Now, after 20 years as a stepmom, I find joy in the long-term benefits of healthy, thriving relationships with my stepchildren that outweigh the unending sacrifices of the early years.

We need God's help during periods of ongoing sacrifice as stepmoms. Recently, I was introduced to a beautiful illustration—Cord of Three Strands. With this unique addition to a wedding ceremony, a couple braids a cord of three strands together to represent God's sacred union. A powerful keepsake, the cord reminds us of God's presence through sacrifice or celebration in marriage.[5]

Prayer: *Heavenly Father, I need Your strength during periods of intense sacrifice. Please sustain me when I grow weary. Thank you for Your unending presence in my life.*

~ Gayla

---

[5]Cord of Three Strands: http://www.godsknot.com/cord-of-three-strands/

Between a Rock and a Hard Place

"Then the Lord said to Moses, 'Tell the Israelites to turn back and encamp near Pi Hahiroth, between Migdol and the sea. They are to encamp by the sea, directly opposite Baal Zephon" (Exodus 14:1-2 NIV).

Thought for the Day: What do you do, when you don't know what to do?

Today's scripture shows God leading the enslaved Israelites out of captivity with a pillar of cloud and fire. They were thrilled with excitement—until. They soon realized He had intentionally led them into a cul-de-sac between monstrous hills and the edge of a sea too deep to be crossed, and too wide to go around. They didn't wander into this peril on their own. His heavenly GPS methodically took them to this spot of vulnerability and danger. Why?

Doesn't being in a stepfamily feel like that sometimes? Don't we occasionally think God played a, "bait-and-switch?" We believed God was providing a way out of our loneliness, shame and depression only to discover a situation consumed by confusion, isolation, and irritation.

The truth is God sometimes intentionally places us in perilous situations so we have no place to turn—but to Him.

"The Lord occasionally does the same thing with us, testing our faith, leading us into hardship, teaching us wisdom, showing us his ways. Our first reaction may be a surge of panic and a sense of alarm, but we must learn to consult the Scriptures for guidance."[6]

I know many stepfamilies that feel like they are on the edge of the Red Sea. They can't turn back, and forging ahead seems impossible. What to do?

At this critical place is wise to acknowledge that the Lord either placed you there, or allowed you to be where you are, for reasons that only He understands. Absolute surrender and total trust is required to survive and thrive.

---

[6] Robert J. Morgan, *God Always Makes a Way*, Nashville, TN, Thomas Nelson, 2001, p 6.

Prayer: *Precious, Father, I do feel like I'm between a rock and a hard place with nowhere to turn for answers. It's very dark right now, and I'm so lost. I choose to trust You. I believe You will provide for me. You led me to this family, and You will make a way for us to flourish and prosper. Show me my role in the journey. Even the ability to believe and trust You, comes from You. Thank you Holy Spirit for Your presence in my life.*

~ Laura

Nourish Your Soul

"Beloved, I pray that all may go well with you and that you may be in good health, as it goes well with your soul" (3 John 1:2 ESV).

Thought for the Day: Self-care isn't selfish. It's survival.

Taking care of you, your marriage, and your family is a balancing act. God's Word tells us we must take care of ourselves before we can be a peace-filled caretaker of others. If you are like me, you know this truth, but you don't always live it.

As women, we are wired to be relational, and most of us naturally have a heart to take care of those around us before we take care of ourselves. But remember, you are a vessel of the Holy Spirit. God wants you to nurture your mind, body, and spirit, to care for the temple where He dwells.

When struggles are plentiful, caring for yourself can seem impossible. If you feel paralyzed with emotional pain, turn to God and let Him work on nourishing your soul. Scripture explains that a merry heart can bring healing. Having a merry heart starts with a focus on Christ and a commitment to care for ourselves as He commands us to do.

A healthy body and mind start with a healthy soul. When you spend time with God and nourish your soul, amazing things happen. You desire to care for your body, and your emotions, too.

Taking care of yourself enables you to better care for your spouse, your marriage, and your family. Serving God with a sound mind and body is a calling we all need to answer.

Prayer: *Dear Heavenly Father, You call me worthy and tell me I am a temple where You dwell. I want to care for myself so I can honor You and care for my husband, my marriage, and my family. Wipe away any notion that self-care is selfish and replace it with a desire to make time to take care of myself. Help me to stay close to You and nurture my soul. Empower me to never forget I am worthy of being cared for.*

~ Heather

Prayer Brings Peace

"Do not be anxious about anything, but in everything, by prayer and petition, with thanksgiving, present your requests to God. And the peace of God, which transcends all understanding, will guard your hearts and your minds in Christ Jesus" (Philippians 4:6-7 NIV).

Thought for the Day: We find peace through prayer.

Words tumbled out of her mouth before I could even say hello. I knew it had been a rough morning for my friend, a new stepmom. As we ordered lunch, I asked about the dispute with her husband.

"We have an ongoing issue with my stepson. At 22 years old, he can't seem to manage his money. My husband wants to bail him out of his financial woes, and I don't agree with it. I've told him I don't support his decision but he's going to do it anyway."

Tears of frustration began to spill down her face. Exasperated by her lack of control, she looked to me for an answer. "What would you do?"

As I reflected on previous disagreements over my stepchildren, I reminded her that we don't always have the final say as stepmoms. "When our husband parents differently than we would, it's OK to tell them we disagree. But then, we have to let it go (short of neglect or abuse). I've learned when I pray about it, I experience peace, regardless of the outcome."

I saw my friend again a few months later. This time, she had a smile on her face. "I've learned to let my husband manage the money issues with his son. I pray for wisdom for his parenting and leave the results up to God. I experience a lot more peace that way."

Prayer: *Dear Lord, thank you for the privilege of prayer. You know my circumstances better than I do. Take the reins of my life and show me how to find peace in the midst of disharmony.*

~ Gayla

Emasculation Leads to Humiliation

"So again I say, each man must love his wife as he loves himself, and the wife must respect her husband" (Ephesians 5:33 NLT).

Thought for the Day: Treating my husband with respect honors God.

When my mom comes to visit sometimes we enter into the confusing mother-daughter, parent-child dance. That's when our roles get blurred. Recently, when this occurred I thought to myself, "She's bossy. It hurts when she speaks to me like that."

God used the situation as a teachable moment. He quickly responded, "That's how your husband feels when you disrespect him, and speak to him like a child."

Ouch!!

But of course, He was right.

Why do I do that? I hate it when I speak to my precious honey in a condescending, critical tone. And yet sometimes I do.

That's when it's time to get alone with God and beg Him to transform my mind. I need to learn new ways to communicate that aren't hurtful and biting. Pushing my sweetheart down — in order to elevate myself — will backfire.

Yes, I need to share my thoughts or feelings with my spouse. I'm not called to be a spineless wimp who tolerates abuse. Setting healthy boundaries is fine. But it's not wise — or productive — if my words (especially those surrounding his parenting skills or the actions of his kids) dominate or emasculate my husband. My job is to build him up with respect and kindness.

Prayer: *Lord, my tongue can be my weakest, and my strongest, body part. You know me very well. Tame my tongue. Help me to think, before I speak. When I'm hurt or angry teach me to count to ten, or twenty, or one hundred, and pray before opening my mouth. I'm desperate.*

~ Laura

I'll Have What She's Having

"...for you are still of the flesh. For while there is jealousy and strife among you, are you not of the flesh and behaving only in a human way?" (1 Corinthians 3:3 ESV).

Thought for the Day: Comparison steals contentment. A grateful heart brings peace to your home.

It's human nature for us to compare ourselves to others. Yet that comparison is a thief of joy. I often recall a plaque that hung on the wall of a former boss: "Contentment isn't having what you want but wanting what you have."

As a naive 21-year-old, while those words didn't speak to me at the time, they did stay with me. I recall them often and remind myself to take solace in the blessings I do have.

If you are in a difficult season in your marriage, it is so easy to get on Facebook or another social media site and see photos of "happy" couples and read mushy words about how wonderful your friend's husband is and how their marriage is "perfect."

While there is no such thing as a marriage void of conflict, when you believe others have one, it can be easy to feel empty and alone. If you find that social media leaves you longing for a different marriage or another type of husband, get off it. Remember, anyone can be anyone online. Often women post what they want in their marriages and in their husbands instead of what they really have.

Trade comparing your marriage, husband, or family to someone else's with desiring what you do have. Focus your time and thoughts on the blessings in your marriage and family and on ways you can improve your contribution to them.

Prayer: *Lord, place a desire in me to treasure my husband, marriage, and family. When I find myself looking at others and wanting what they have, remind me that I am right where You call me to be. May I find peace in knowing I am living out the plan You have for me and that You will never leave nor forsake me. Guide me through my day and remove any temptation to compare what I have with another. You are more than enough, Jesus, and may I live in that truth each and every day.*

~ Heather

Letting Go of Control

"...'Everything is permissible for me,' but I will not be brought under the control of anything" (1 Corinthians 6:12 HCSB).

Thought for the Day: When I learn to accept what I cannot change, I find peace.

I tend to be a control freak. It's not a good thing — especially if you live in a stepfamily.

For years I tried to control everything. My husband's behavior toward my girls, the relationship between my kids and my stepkids, our ex-spouses' decisions, my stepkids' feelings toward me... I could go on and on.

I was driving my family and myself crazy. I needed to change. One day I found Reinhold Niebuhr's Serenity Prayer and knew it was the answer. "God grant me the serenity to accept the things I cannot change, courage to change the things I can, and the wisdom to know the difference."

I couldn't believe the peace I felt as I determined to focus on what I could control and let go of what I couldn't. I couldn't control the back and forth schedule that might change on a whim, but I could make alternate plans for important dates. I couldn't speed up the relationship bonding I desired between my children and my stepchildren, but I could encourage kind and considerate behavior toward one another.

As I learned to accept what I couldn't change, often lowering my expectations of a situation, I found peace and contentment.

Prayer: *Jesus, I need Your help to let go of the things I'm trying to control. Give me courage to accept what I cannot change and strength to change the things I can. I can't do this alone.*

~ Gayla

New Traditions

"Therefore, if anyone is in Christ, the new creation has come: The old has gone, the new is here!" (2 Corinthians 5:17 NIV).

Thought for the Day: Stop focusing on the past. Start something new.

As a stepmom it's easy to get caught in the trap of trying to duplicate what the kids have or do at the other home. But making new traditions, especially during the special occasions or holidays can go a long way toward bonding the stepfamily.

Here are some favorite stepmom suggestions for new things to try:

- Place a basket in front of each person, family members write what's special about that person on a 3x5 card and places in his/her basket. Then go around the room reading each one.
- Buy a Christmas ornament that represents a new trip, place or vacation. Reminisce over that trip as you decorate the Christmas tree.
- Have a theme meal, (ex: Mexican, Chinese, Italian) talk about what it might be like to visit that country.
- For Fall: A hayride, cookie exchange, driving to see the lights, ice skating, or a hockey game can be a new stepfamily adventure.
- Fondue, where each child gets to pick a fruit, bread or veggie to cut up and dip away!

Brainstorm. It's fun. If you aren't Martha Stewart or it doesn't look like a page out of Southern Living Magazine don't worry about it! The key is to keep it simple, loving, and a new tradition that connects your family.

Prayer: *Lord, help me to refrain from trying to become something I'm not. In particular help me to stop competing with the biological mom's gifts or skills. You created me with unique talents. Allow me to be a blessing to my family and at peace just as I am.*

~ Laura

One Step Forward, Sixteen Steps Back: Loving at Their Pace

"Every good and perfect gift is from above, coming down from the Father of the heavenly lights, who does not change like shifting shadows" (James 1:17 NIV).

Thought for the Day: Steprelationships have their own unique pace. Keep in step with God and He will direct your path.

"What's the point?" Sherry sobbed. "I try and try to build a relationship with my stepson and it seems the more I try the more he pushes back. I give up."

This stepmom's discouragement is common. Steprelationships have both progress and setbacks.

I share Sherry's struggle when it comes to the relationships I have with my stepdaughters. We can be making progress and the next thing I know it feels we've gone backward. One day I hear, "I'm so glad you're here for me," and the next day, "I want my mom doing that! Not you. Leave me alone!"

Stepfamilies are built on loss, and the memory of that loss is triggered by different things for different people. When it is, stepkids can often respond by reacting to their stepparent. I work at treating my two stepdaughters the same, yet we have different relationships. Each relationship is defined by my stepchild, not by me.

Don't take it personally if one day it appears you have made great progress with a stepchild and the next day it seems you are starting over. This is normal. Continue to love in God's strength and know that one of the greatest gifts you can give is the gift of being consistent in your presence and care.

It's important to remember that feelings are not truth. Just because you feel your relationship has gone backward does not mean it actually has. I have spoken with so many adult stepchildren who've said that growing up they were very hard on their stepmothers because they felt they weren't allowed to "like" them as it might hurt their moms. Age enabled them to see the love and constant care their stepmoms provided and to treasure her presence and blessings later in their lives.

Prayer: *Dear Heavenly Father, I love You and I desire to have a healthy relationship with my stepkids. You are in control of our relationships. Regardless how close I feel to them or how distant, I will not be defined by it. I seek to live in You as You live in me.*

~ Heather

Unanswered Questions

"So do not fear, for I am with you; do not be dismayed, for I am your God. I will strengthen you and help you; I will uphold you with My righteous right hand" (Isaiah 41:10 NIV).

Thought for the Day: I find strength for the journey as I live one day at a time.

As I write this, my brother-in-law lies in a hospital bed in ICU. Last week he's a perfectly healthy 54-year-old man running his own business. Suddenly he turns up critically ill with dangerously high fever and low blood pressure. How does that happen? Will he recover?

The doctors have no answers.

Have you ever felt that way in your stepfamily? One day you're cruising on auto-pilot, beginning to enjoy more harmony in your relationships, when all of a sudden your stepchild begins to show disrespect and hatred with every interaction. Or perhaps your generally cooperative ex-spouse refuses to negotiate any kind of change with the visitation schedule. Questions without answers abound.

Our family experienced an unexpected custody battle with one of our children that didn't make sense to my husband or me. A cloud of confusion parked above my head as I walked through long, difficult days. I wanted immediate answers but found more questions with each passing day. During that time, I learned to focus on one day at a time, seeking the Lord for direction, but refusing to project what tomorrow might bring.

Prayer: *Heavenly Father, help me stay focused on today when I have unanswered questions about tomorrow. Thank you for making my paths straight.*

~ Gayla

Fear: The Thief of Life

"Fear not, for I am with you; Be not dismayed, for I am your God. I will strengthen you, Yes, I will help you, I will uphold you with My righteous right hand" (Isaiah 41:10 NKJV).

Thought for the Day: God is my *only* source of strength.

"Laura, your brain MRI is abnormal," the doctor calmly stated. "The scar tissue likely means an auto immune disease such as multiple sclerosis."

I was in shock. My mind whirled, "How could this be? I feel fine. I don't even take any medicine. No! No! NO! This isn't possible."

As the weeks went by, and the reality that I might have a crippling disease danced in my brain, so did the fangs of fear.

The devious arrows of panic taunted and satan droned, "How's that 'God-thing' working for you now, little Laura? Steve will die and with no kids of your own, your last days will be in a wheelchair as a lonely, pathetic, old lady who can't even wipe her own butt. That's your future! So much for 'Jesus loves me, this I know' Ha!"

If you are a stepmom without biological kids it's easy to wonder if you'll end up alone, without support. Guess what? Moms with biological kids can end up alone, and sometimes stepkids *do* take care of an aging stepmom. Life provides no guarantees.

My final diagnosis was that I had a stroke, it wasn't MS. Regardless, we must fight the fear of the unknown and lean on the only source that never changes — Jesus Christ. He is my provider. He never leaves. He never sleeps. He never changes. He never fails.

Prayer: *Holy God, this is Your little girl crying out. Teach me how to replace fears and lies with the truth that in Your arms I'm safe. Whether I'm ill or healthy, widowed or married, happy or sad, young or old, rich or poor, You see me only as Your precious daughter. Thank you for loving me. Amen.*

~ Laura

Vintage Thinking

"Give thanks to Him who led His people through the wilderness. His faithful love endures forever" (Psalm 136:16 NLT).

Thought for the Day: Open your heart and mind to different views while standing strong in the truth that is God.

While black-and-white movies are a favorite of mine, black-and-white thinking is not. I'll admit, when I first married my husband, I was a black-and-white thinker, and he was, too.

We were two "successful" single parents when we met, and we agreed on the kind of children we wanted to raise—healthy, compassionate, responsible kids who were honest, accountable, and had a strong faith in God. You can imagine how excited we were to find out we had the same values. We figured blending our two families would be easy. We loved each other. Our kids liked each other. Our kids liked the person we were preparing to marry. AND we both wanted the same things for our kids.

There was one minor factor we hadn't discussed—our individual parenting styles. Unbeknownst to us, we had different ideas and dissimilar approaches to getting at the same goal. Our "we are going to be like the Brady Bunch minus Alice" mentality was wiped off the board when we discovered we not only disagreed on ways to raise our kids, but also on consequences for their actions.

In order to come to center, we both had to let go of our black-and-white thinking that there was one right way of doing things when raising our kids. We worked hard to learn to blend our styles and to think in shades of gray, acknowledging that there may be more than one way to do things. We had to ask and answer the question, "Do I want to be right or do I want to be right in my marriage?" The answer opened our eyes to different options and the opportunity to support one another.

Prayer: *Dear Heavenly Father, when my husband and I are at a disagreement on kid issues, help us to seek You and to think how we can work together instead of pushing our own way of doing things. Give me peace and help me support my husband even when I don't agree with Him. May the decisions we make in our home reflect our faith in You and may we guide our children on a path that points them heaven-bound.*

~ Heather

It's Okay to Grieve

"The Lord is close to the brokenhearted and saves those who are crushed in spirit" (Psalm 34:18 NIV).

Thought for the Day: God comforts us, often in unique ways, when we ask and expect to receive.

I couldn't stop the tears that spilled down my cheeks as I drove away from my parent's house. I had spent the day with my mom and could clearly see dementia stealing a part of her personality day by day. No longer the mom who raised me, I grieved the relationship we would never have again.

God wants to walk through the valley of grief with us, but we must ask for His help. As I left my parent's house and cried out to the Lord, He sent his angels to comfort me through my three sisters. Although my siblings and I live in four different states, we communicate often. My youngest sister called first to ask how my visit went. While on the phone with her, my oldest sister called. Before I could hang up, my other sister called. God prompted their calls in the middle of the day to encourage me during my moment of sadness.

Grief plays an undeniable role in our stepfamily relationships also. It's not unusual to experience difficult years in the beginning, full of conflict and angst, as new relationships come together. When we don't experience the white-picket fence family we had dreamed of, sadness sets in.

Prayer: *Heavenly Father, I don't like feeling sad. But sometimes I'm consumed with grief, as I feel overwhelmed by my challenges. Please help me feel Your comforting presence today.*

~ Gayla

The Blind Spots

"So all of us who have had that veil removed can see and reflect the glory of the Lord. And the Lord — who is the Spirit — makes us more and more like him as we are changed into his glorious image" (2 Corinthians 3:18 NLT).

Thought for the Day: Who have I allowed to speak truth into my life without fear of retaliation?

"He is well loved by many, but well-liked by few," my friend stated about a Christian ministry leader. "He is extremely difficult to work with, and he won't listen to constructive criticism."

It became obvious that although this leader was passionate about Jesus, he had glaring blind spots that were apparent to those around him.

Afterwards, I was perplexed. How could such a godly person have such huge character flaws? Why didn't the Holy Spirit convict him? What's broken here?

And then it hit me. This man didn't allow even one person into his life to hold him accountable. A holy chill ran through my bones and I pondered, "What about me?"

Humbly I asked, "God, are there negative things in my life that are obvious to everyone else, but I refuse to see them? Show me, Holy Spirit."

This is why it's crucial for a stepmom to have a nourishing support group. It's very easy to become so embroiled in our own stepfamily drama and perspective that a fresh observation from another stepmom may be needed.

The question is: Who holds you accountable? Have you placed yourself in a setting where there is at least one good friend who can tell you something unpleasant? Are you ready to remove the blinders that may be hindering your next step as a stepmom?

Prayer: *Dear God, please place wise, mature women in my path that will be courageous enough to tell me when I'm wrong. Give me a humble heart and a teachable mind so that blind spots don't block my spiritual vision. Remind me that when I avoid accountability that it affects my future, my husband, my friends and my family. Thank you for patiently pointing out the things that are poor choices. Jesus, You are a good friend to me. Amen*

~ Laura

Looking Through the Stepmom Lens

"Do not conform to the pattern of this world, but be transformed by the renewing of your mind. Then you will be able to test and approve what God's will is — his good, pleasing and perfect will" (Romans 12:2 NIV).

Thought for the Day: A parent and stepparent can look at the same child and see something different. The lens you look through determines the view you see.

Have you ever shared concerns regarding your stepchild with your spouse only to be met with opposition? Has your heart ever crumbled when your spouse fails to see your good intentions to help? Have you ever wondered if you are going crazy because you and your spouse tend to see your stepchild two different ways? If you answered yes to any of these questions, please know you are not alone.

I have determined that it is the lens through which a parent and a stepparent view a child that makes the difference in how they relate. A biological or adoptive parent looks at a child first through the lens of love. A stepparent first sees through the lens of responsibility. The view can be different.

Understanding this truth about stepfamilies made a HUGE difference in how I brought things to my husband regarding his kids and how he brought things to me regarding mine. This helped me to understand why his reactions to certain behaviors were so much different than mine.

I had the best intentions when I brought him concerns regarding my stepkids, but my lens of responsibility clashed with his lens of love. Instead of dealing with the behavioral issues, our discussions quickly became about how I didn't understand his children or how he was blind to what was going on.

As you can imagine, I became defensive and he became defensive. I was defending my intentions and he was defending his perceptions. The truth is, they will never line up. Responsibility and love are two different views. They are parallel, but don't intersect in the beginning of a stepfamily.

Prayer: *Lord, help both my husband and me to see our children through Your lens of grace. When my husband and I are in conflict, please convict us to seek You. Our view of the kids doesn't determine their future — only You do that. Help us to see each other through a lens of love, grace, and mercy, and to look at the kids with those same godly eyes.*

~ Heather

Risking Love

"My grace is sufficient for you, for my power is made perfect in weakness. Therefore I will boast all the more gladly about my weaknesses, so that Christ's power may rest on me" (2 Corinthians 12:9 NIV).

Thought for the Day: God's power overcomes our hurts. We can dare to love again.

Words from the voice on the radio played over in my head, piercing my heart. "We must dare to love those who hurt us." The hurt from my gaping wound lay open. A friend I thought I could trust had let me down. I didn't want to consider that I should dare to love her again.

I recognized the feeling from another time. Hurt by words of one of my stepchildren, I found it easier to guard my heart than make myself vulnerable to love again. I learned that a heart with walls around it, however, never experiences joy or peace.

With the Lord's help, I reached out to my friend and offered forgiveness. Recognizing God's grace of my own sin softened my heart toward my friend.

We can dare to love again even if we've been hurt. Risking love is worth the gamble.

Prayer: *Heavenly Father, thank you for Your promise of abundant grace and power. May Your Spirit overwhelm me in my weakness.*

~ Gayla

Tomatoes in My Ice Cream

"A man who refuses to admit his mistakes can never be successful. But if he confesses and forsakes them, he gets another chance" (Proverbs 28:13 TLB).

Thought for the Day: It's best to admit—sometimes I'm wrong.

My mom loves to tell the story about the time when five-year-old little Laura started screaming at an ice cream parlor. The outburst resulted after my mother foolishly decided to replace my regular boring vanilla cone with cherry vanilla.

Big mistake.

I wanted those tomatoes out of my ice cream—immediately!!

She could not convince me, no matter how hard she tried, that the red spots were cherries and not tomatoes. Because I was wrong, I missed out on a luscious new treat. And my mother ended up eating two ice cream cones that day.

As a stepmom I'm often wrong. I've learned it's not such a bad thing. It's best just to humble myself, admit it, say I'm sorry, and repent. True remorse requires taking steps toward change. That means learning new ways to communicate, cope, or respond.

Letting go of the need to always be right can offer such freedom. However, accepting my human frailty is not a "get out of jail free" card, or an excuse for hurting others with comments such as "that's just the way I am."

The wise stepmom knows that when she turns her mistakes into an opportunity for growth, everyone benefits.

Now, I think it's time for a little Baskin-Robbins. Cherry vanilla, of course!!

Prayer: *Holy God, You never make mistakes. That makes me all the more grateful when You forgive me when I do. I desire to learn how to graciously and meekly admit an error, and then let it go. It doesn't mean I'm always wrong, it merely means I made a poor choice. Teach me to forgive myself, and become whole again. Amen.*

~ Laura

God Is in the Business of Restoration

"Look straight ahead, and fix your eyes on what lies before you" (Proverbs 4:25 NLT).

Thought for the Day: God makes all things new and He can restore your marriage.

"I miss feeling loved," a stepmom whispered to me on a coaching call. "I miss feeling like I matter to my husband. I've been reduced to a cook, maid, and sex partner. I'm so empty inside."

This stepmom was desperate and she wanted me to tell her how to fix it. I shared how to find peace but it wasn't the answer she wanted. "Seek Christ to fill you. Fix your eyes on Him alone and listen to His voice," I advised. "If your husband is being un-Christ-like, confront him in love and then leave it with him and pray for God to convict him. Do not compare your marriage to others, but instead, seek to be filled by God's love and be loving toward your husband."

My heart weeps for all the stepmothers who have a deep ache for the husband and marriage they once had or wish they had.

The truth is, remarriage is hard. Struggles invade our hearts and couples can slowly drift apart. But know this: God is bigger than any struggle you face and He is mighty to save. He is a God of restoration and redemption. He can fully restore your marriage and make it more than you ever dreamed.

The next time you feel alone and empty, run to God. When you hear a voice inside tell you, "You are only a ____ to your husband," replace it with God's voice. You are complete in Him. He says you are worthy. Believe this to be true.

Prayer: *Dear Heavenly Father, I ask You to fill me with peace and hope about my husband. I feel so empty inside and miss the man I married and the love we used to share. I don't want to give the struggles in our lives power, but rather, to believe all power and control rest in You. May my heart remain loving toward my husband and may I not give up hope for our marriage. Help me to nurture our relationship and have full confidence that You are in control and will guide us together and forward as we seek to follow You.*

~ Heather

Loving My Stepchildren

"My command is this: Love each other as I have loved you" (John 15:12 NIV).

Thought for the Day: Feelings for our stepchildren often change with time.

"I love my own children differently than I love my stepchildren, and I feel so guilty about it." My friend, Sarah, voiced the feelings of many stepmoms.

We develop a bond unlike any when we give birth to our children, nurse them for months, and experience every first with them. It's not unusual to love our stepchildren differently. In fact, in the early years, we might not love — or even like them — some days.

I needed God's help in loving my stepchildren in the beginning. I wanted to offer them the same grace I freely gave my biological children, but it didn't come naturally for me. I prayed I would see them through His eyes, not mine. My heart began to soften as I prayed for my stepchildren by name.

Stepfamily relationships may always feel a little different than biological ones. But don't be surprised if, with each passing year, you notice a growing love toward your stepchild.

Prayer: *Thank you Father for loving me on days I'm not lovable. Show me how to see my stepchildren as You see them, and love them in the midst of confusing emotions.*

~ Gayla

Special Occasions: Diffusing the Triggers

"God, who knows the heart, showed that He accepted them by giving the Holy Spirit to them, just as He did to us" (Acts 15:8 NIV).

Thought for the Day: On my own strength I will fall. The Holy Spirit resides in me, He provides the power.

During the early years of my remarriage there was many a Christmas when I wanted to sneak out to the manger scene in my freezing front yard and ask Baby Jesus to move over. I badly needed some "heavenly peace" and a nap.

There is nothing quite like a special occasion such as a: holiday, wedding, graduation or birthday party, to trigger stepfamily tension. So what's a stepmom to do?

Take the high ground; don't be ambushed by the complexities, and pray—a lot!

In other words, don't be naïve about the situation and learn how to think and react like Jesus. The good news is we don't have the ability to do that on our own strength. Hallelujah! When a person accepts Jesus as the Savior, the Holy Spirit takes up residence. It's HIS job to produce the joy, peace, patience, goodness, self-control and kindness that can ooze from us.

Our first job is to abide, or cling to Christ. We do this by reading God's Word, prayer, and staying close to mature believers. This is how the Holy Spirit teaches and transforms us. The second is to surrender our words, responses, actions, reactions so that they reflect those of Christ.

I'm amazed at how quickly and smoothly the Holy Spirit will fill my mind and heart with His thoughts and wisdom. It majestically happens when I extinguish the need to be right, and I just want Jesus.

Prayer: *Holy God, a special occasion is coming and to be honest I'm dreading it. I'd rather run away than face the drama. But I trust You. Holy Spirit, God's Word says You live in me. And that Your role is to make me more like Christ. On my own this can get very ugly, so I surrender.*

~ Laura

Guardian of My Heart

"...and the peace of God, which surpasses all understanding, will guard your hearts and minds through Christ Jesus" (Philippians 4:7 NKJV).

Thought for the Day: A difficult season in your marriage does not define it. Seeing things from your spouse's perspective can bring hope, comfort and strength.

There was a time when I questioned my decision to remarry. My husband and I would get tangled up in kid and ex-spouse issues and resolution seemed impossible. I love my husband, but during those times, I didn't like him or what was happening to us.

While my feet wanted to walk, my heart stayed still. I reached the point where I believed my husband could not hear me or my good intentions. My only option for change was prayer.

Ironically, it was soaking in prayer that gave me a peace that transcended my circumstances. I should not have felt peaceful. But I did. As someone prone to depression, I could have been in a deep one. But I wasn't.

In those hours, drenched in prayer and Bible reading, God's words came alive to me. I no longer just read words on a page. I lived them. I began to see myself through Christ's eyes and to place my hope in Him alone. I lived the blessing of being still and loving my husband in Christ's strength.

During that time, I was struggling with discerning between being a godly wife and being a doormat. The Lord literally guarded my heart and mind from asking, "What if we don't make it," because I trusted that we would.

When I opened myself in complete surrender to God, He opened my eyes to my husband's pain and what was guiding him. I saw that the hurt my husband felt over the chaos his daughter created in our home had taken a heavy toll on him. Just as I was feeling hurt and alone, so was my husband. God replaced the hurt and sadness I felt toward my husband with compassion. I made a commitment to love him through any challenges with grace and respect.

Prayer: *Dear Heavenly Father, there are times when I look at my husband and wonder where the man I married has gone. He seems worn out and angry. Give me eyes to see his pain. Help me to nurture our marriage and make it a safe place for him to share his struggles. Lord, You designed me to honor and respect my husband, yet sometimes I don't want to. Give me the desire to be a godly wife and discern when I should put up boundaries and when I should break them down. Help me to love him as You do.*

~ Heather

Count Your Blessings

"Give thanks to the LORD, for he is good; His love endures forever" (1 Chronicles 16:34 NIV).

Thought for the Day: We find joy when we count our blessings.

My heart sank. "Gayla, I'm on hospice. Come see me if you can." I had to re-read my friend's text. Although Dotty had been battling cancer, I wasn't ready to admit she had only days left on this earth. She was like a second mother to me. I attended her weekly prayer group for almost a decade while my blended family trudged through a difficult season.

Staring at her text, I made plans to travel out of state so I could say goodbye. Thankful for Dotty's influence, I wanted to tell her the blessing she'd been to me.

I stood by her bedside for the last time. While tears filled my eyes, I expressed my heartfelt love and praise. I recounted years of praying through challenges and watching God's hand at work. We laughed and cried and sang and prayed. It was a beautiful afternoon with a special friend. But soon, it was time to leave. I would have to say my last goodbye. As I leaned over to kiss her beautifully aged skin, I lingered. "I love you. I'll see you again someday." I choked out the words before I left her room. I walked away, tears streaming down my face.

As I drove home the next day, I thanked God for a special friendship. Dotty's prayers had given me strength for my stepparenting journey when I didn't know if I could keep going. Her encouragement led me to believe in myself when I wanted to give up. As I counted my blessings, even amidst intense sadness, God gave me joy.

Prayer: *Heavenly Father, give me a thankful heart. Help me find joy, even amidst heartache, as I count my many blessings. Thank you for Your constant presence during times of difficulty.*

~ Gayla

Who's In Charge?

"She brings him good, not harm, all the days of her life" (Proverbs 31:12 NIV).

Thought for the Day: Has fear caused me to step in to a place that is best to avoid?

Sometimes a stepfamily gets into trouble because there isn't a strong leader. The Bible explains that a healthy marriage requires the husband to be the head of the home. It can be hard for today's woman to understand her husband's role, especially if she grew up in a hurting or broken family. For that woman the image and definition of headship may have been perverted into: dictator, manipulator, deserter or bully. These are not the characteristics of a wise, humble, godly leader.

"Leadership ability is the lid on the success of a nation or organization. When Israel or Judah lived under good kings, things went well. Under bad kings, things went sour. The heart and skill of a leader will always tremendously affect the life of the people under his direction. This is a law, both timeless and universal."[7]

In a stepfamily marriage it can be even more confusing to discern "Who's in charge?" A divorce sometimes leaves a man plagued by guilt, shame and lethargy. And a father who parents from those unhealthy emotions produces turmoil and chaos in his home.

A smart stepmom knows that her role isn't to usurp her husband's authority and position, but rather to gently guide and help him find his place. This might include: classes on parenting, a mentor or life coach, a marriage retreat or other resources that can teach him the proper way to be the head of his home.

When equipped, many men will step up to the plate and let go of the shouting, force, laziness or apathy that plagues so many homes today. When a wife observes a loving husband who is hungry to become a godly, wise leader she can relax and let go. It doesn't happen overnight.

God is graciously patient when a man desires to become a good husband and father.

---

[7] http://www.iequip.org/daily-devotional/as-the-leader-goes-so-goes-the-nation

Prayer: *Lord, I admit it. I like to be in control. Actually, I'm afraid when I'm not in control. But the desire of my heart is to let YOU be in control. It's not my job to teach my husband how to lead. That's between him and You. It is my job to get out of the way, and relinquish the leadership role. Both of us can't stand in the same spot. Help me, Lord, to trust You so that I can trust my husband to be the head of our home.*

~ Laura

Living Under the Microscope

"There is therefore now no condemnation for those who are in Christ Jesus" (Romans 8:1 ESV).

Thought for the Day: You can't fight crazy but you can go crazy trying.

As a stepmom you can find yourself in a no-win situation when it comes to the ex-wife and stepkids. If you are loving toward your stepkids you can be accused of stepping on their mom's toes. And if you insist they call you by your first name some people would say you are being cold.

Focus on doing what is right and what you and your husband agree on in regard to mothering. When I've been accused of overstepping my bounds, I've stated that I treat even strangers and guests who come into my home with love, acceptance, and compassion so I am surely not going to give my stepchildren any less.

It can feel no-win when you are living under a microscope. Exhaustion and anxiety can overwhelm you as you over-think every decision out of fear of what the "other" home will say about you.

You cannot prevent your stepkids, their mom, or outsiders from criticizing you. But you can always remember the truth from God. You are worthy. You are loved. Your worth does not depend on another person, but on the One who made you.

This truth doesn't take away the pain of being criticized, but it does remind you that their opinion doesn't determine your destination in life. When drama comes knocking on your door, choose not to answer it. Often the best response is silence. God knows the truth and He will defend you and love you. His love is never dependent upon how another sees you.

Prayer: *Lord, some days I am so wounded by hurtful words or actions by my stepkids or their mother. Help me to take that hurt captive and replace it with Your truth. Remove from me a need to respond. Keep me calm and centered. Remind me that truth is truth and it can't be changed because another person wants to twist it. May I find rest and peace in Your unconditional love for me.*

~ Heather

Where to Find Hope

"May the God of hope fill you with all joy and peace as you trust in him, so that you may overflow with hope by the power of the Holy Spirit" (Romans 15:13 NIV).

Thought for the Day: God's Word gives us hope, as we trust in Him.

An unwed pregnancy. Repeated struggles with addiction. Defiant behavior. The stepmom sitting across from me had been through it all and more with her teenage stepdaughter. I had watched her come out on the other side with a stronger faith and hope for better days. But I knew it hadn't been easy.

I talk to a lot of stepmoms, each with a unique story. I often hear details of heartache, disappointment, frustration, or unmet expectations. Some relay victory after months or years of a disjointed journey. Others are still walking through the fire. Through each account I've noticed one thing in common that propels them through difficulty—hope.

Where do you find hope? Many turn to unhealthy relationships, addictions, or the lure of materialism. But true hope only comes from God.

When my husband lost his job, we didn't know where the funds would come from to help our three kids in college. It wasn't the first time we had struggled financially in the midst of raising five kids. In fact, finances had been tight a lot! But I could always find hope by trusting in God's promises.

God's Word always encourages me. I have to take time to read it, meditate on it, and pray over it, however, to apply it to my circumstances and find hope for the future.

Prayer: *Dear Lord, thank you for Your promises of hope in Scripture. Please plant them in my heart during times of struggle.*

~ Gayla

My Achy-Breaky Heart

"Praise be to the God and Father of our Lord Jesus Christ, the Father of compassion and the God of all comfort, who comforts us in all our troubles, so that we can comfort those in any trouble with the comfort we ourselves receive from God" (2 Corinthians 1:3-4 NIV).

Thought for the Day: A stepmom can become a safe place to fall.

"It absolutely breaks my heart when the biological mom says she will be there for my stepdaughter and then she doesn't show up," stepmom Ariel cried. "She has done this numerous times. I don't know what to do when she keeps breaking her heart over and over again."

One of the hardest parts about being a stepparent is watching a stepchild's pain caused by the actions or poor choices of a biological parent. And there is no easy answer.

It's vitally important for the stepmom to understand that because she isn't the person causing the wound, she can't completely heal it. That's the hard part. On the other hand she can be a, "soft place to fall." In other words she can be a conduit of encouragement, comfort, love and strength to a hurting child. Her gentle, kind words of affirmation and compassion can go a long way toward helping the child feel loved and safe.

Words such as, "I'm so sorry you are hurting. I know you wanted your mom to be there so badly. It's normal to want a parent there to see us, and my heart is aching for you. I know it doesn't take the pain away but always know your dad and I are so proud of you. I'm honored that you are my stepdaughter, and I brag about you to everyone."

Just knowing another human being "sees my pain and cares" can bring healing.

Resist the temptation to spew slanderous comments such as, "Your mother is an idiot for not attending." Bashing the mother will backfire on the father or stepmom and harm the child. What the child hears is, "Your mother is an idiot and you are a part of her, which means you are an idiot too."

Prayer: *Holy God, You have placed this precious life into my care. I'm unworthy and often afraid. Help me to be a vessel of Your peace, grace, and love. Let the words of my mouth bring healing and encouragement to this treasured hurting soul. Give me wisdom.*

~ Laura

Who Is the Woman in the Mirror?

"Casting all your care upon Him, for He cares for you" (1 Peter 5:7 NKJV).

Thought for the Day: Don't allow yourself to get lost in the struggles of stepfamily life.

It was like any other morning. I was putting on makeup and curling my hair when I stopped to really see myself in the mirror. Instead of the vibrant, fun-loving woman I used to be, an exhausted, lonely, sad woman stared back at me. I hardly recognized my reflection.

What was happening? This was more than the inevitable, natural aging process. Although I'd tried to pretend life was wonderful, I knew something more was evident in that reflection. The stress and strain of stepfamily living and all the challenges we faced were taking a toll. My face was revealing the pain, confusion and sorrow I was too embarrassed to confess.

In that moment, I realized I had been giving all my energy to battles that weren't mine to fight. Battles that, as part of a blended family, had no victories.

Over time, I have learned to cast my cares upon the Lord, helping me to find release of pressure and pain. I have come to terms with the fact that there are some things I cannot change. I have the freedom to fight but when I do, it is often myself and my marriage that loses.

Prayer: *Dear Heavenly Father, help me to cast my cares upon You fully. Convict my hurting heart to give them to You and leave them with You. So often I want to pick them up and do things my own way but that only leaves me frustrated and exhausted. Thank you for loving me enough to carry my burdens. They are where they belong — in Your hands, not in mine. Help me to believe that and live it.*

~ Heather

When I Feel Like an Outsider

"…Our purpose is to please God, not people. He alone examines the motives of our hearts" (1 Thessalonians 2:4 NLT).

Thought for the Day: I can't force my stepchildren to let me into their inner circle. But I can be content anyway, finding gratitude in other places of acceptance.

"I feel invisible in my own home." I could see the pain in my friend's eyes. "My husband and stepchildren know how to do life without me, and I often feel excluded. I don't know how to break into the inner circle that surrounds them."

Nodding in agreement, I reflected on my own feelings as an outsider in our early years. I remember the heartache when my family told jokes I didn't understand, reminisced about past experiences I wasn't part of, or left me out of their activity.

Finally, I decided I would accept that some days I had to live with the outsider role. I couldn't force my stepchildren to let me into their inner circle. But I could take care of myself when the feelings of loneliness set in. On those days, I called a friend to go to coffee, caught up on my Bible study, or hit the gym for a workout with my buddies. By engaging in activities outside the home, places where I had my own identity, I better coped with the loneliness I felt at home.

Thankful to call myself an insider in God's family, I'm unconditionally loved and accepted in God's kingdom. I'm also an insider with my family of origin, my biological kids, the couple relationship with my husband, and my profession as a writer. When I recognize my insider status in other areas, I cope better when I'm left out of the circle at home.

Prayer: *Dear Lord, thank you for accepting me into Your kingdom as Your child. Help me focus on You when I feel displaced in my home.*

~ Gayla

Comfort in the Uncomfortable

"The faithful love of the Lord never ends! His mercies never cease. Great is his faithfulness; His mercies begin afresh each morning" (Lamentations 3:22-23 NLT).

Thought for the Day: God is good — All the time.

Living in Florida you occasionally have to put up with tropical "friends" such as snakes or lizards. Normally, they stay in their own habitat — until. One particular day a lizard found its way into my dining room, and Laura immediately turned into Zena, the Warrior Princess. With broom in hand, and the front door wide open, I ever so swiftly swooshed him out to green grass paradise.

I'm sure to him my broom's bristles communicated, "This is the end," when in reality they were his vehicle to safety and freedom.
God is just like that.

When He has to move me out of my comfort zone, it feels like an interruptive push. If I don't fight Him, and I allow His mighty ways to move me, the discomfort eventually lends itself to victory over my situation.

When a stepmom chooses to mature, she discovers that God's holy nudges always move her in the right direction. And that Jesus wants her to be healed, content, successful and thriving in her role even more than she does.

Although the initial push means temporary discomfort, the outcome is productive. Primarily I often resist the process, but I love the results.

Today, are you sensing a "holy poke" from God? Your response can change everything.

Prayer: *Precious Papa, teach me to recognize and submit to Your holy nudge. I want to cease striving. Even though it may be unpleasant in the moment, I desire to let go and allow You to make me like You, even if it means a swift swoosh.*

~ Laura

ABOUT THE AUTHOR

Laura Petherbridge is an international author, speaker and life coach who serves couples and single adults on topics such as: relationships, stepfamilies, co-parenting, single parenting, divorce prevention, and divorce recovery.

She is the author of, *"When I Do" Becomes "I Don't" – Practical Steps for Healing During Separation and Divorce, 101Tips for The Smart Stepmom – Expert Advice from One Stepmom to Another*, and *The Smart Stepmom*, co-authored with stepfamily expert Ron Deal and endorsed by Gary Chapman (*The Five Love Languages*).

In addition to the US she has spoken in Australia, South Africa, and England. Her various speaking engagements, TV and radio broadcasts include:

- The Billy Graham Training Center
- *Family Talk with Dr. James Dobson*
- *Focus on the Family* with Jim Daly
- *Family Life Today* with Dennis Rainey
- Moody Broadcasting
- Lifeway Conference
- MOPS International Conference
- Hearts at Home with Jill Savage
- *The Joni Lamb Show* (Daystar)

In addition to her books she has been published in:

- *Focus on the Family Magazine*

- *Today's Christian Woman*
- Christianity Today's *Marriage Partnership*
- Crosswalk.com and Christian Broadcasting Network (CBN.com)
- *Proverbs 31 Woman* (Lysa Terkeurst)
- Lifeway's *Mature Living*
- *Family Matters*
- *Stepmom Magazine* (Secular)

Laura is a featured expert on the DivorceCare DVD series, which has equipped more than 14,000 churches worldwide. She is the founder of Sisterhood of Stepmoms, a ministry to stepfamilies.

Laura and her pastor husband of 30 years, Steve, reside in Florida. She has two married stepsons that have blessed her with two grandkids.

ABOUT THE AUTHOR

Gayla Grace writes, speaks and coaches on family and stepfamily issues with a desire to educate and empower stepparents, single parents and biological parents in their respective roles. She holds a master's degree in Psychology and Counseling and founded Stepparenting With Grace to offer resources and encouragement to stepfamilies.

She is a monthly columnist for Lifeway's *Parenting Teens*, writing the single parenting and blended family column. She has also been published in more than 75 parenting publications across the United States and Canada including:

- *HomeLife* (Lifeway)
- *Thriving Family* (Focus on the Family)
- *Calgary's Child*
- *Nashville Parent*
- *Atlanta Parent*
- *Alaska Parent*
- *San Diego Family* Magazine
- *South Florida Parenting*
- *Chicago Suburban Family Magazine*
- *Sacramento Parent*
- *New York Parenting*
- *Simply Family Magazine*
- *Little Rock Family*
- *Ithaca Child*
- *Birmingham Parent*
- *Stepmom Magazine*

She is the co-author of *Unwrapping the Gift of Stepfamily Peace* and is contributed to the following books:

- *Stepping with Purpose*
- *101 Tips for the Smart Stepmom*

She has also been published in *Proverbs 31 Woman* (Lysa Terkeurst) and was a monthly column writer for *Women's Inc.* for three years.

Gayla serves on the speaker team with Sisterhood of Stepmoms and speaks at women's events and other stepfamily conferences. Her radio broadcasts include:

- *FamilyLife Today*
- *MomLife Today*
- *Coparenting 101* with Deesha Philyaw

Gayla and her husband, Randy, have five children in their blended family and reside in Shreveport, Louisiana with an "ours" child still at home. She can be reached at www.StepparentingWithGrace.com.

ABOUT THE AUTHOR

Heather Hetchler, M.A. is a writer, speaker, and positive thinker! She is the mom of four and the full-time stepmom of two living in the trenches with all six at home. She is a life coach for stepmothers and the founder of CafeSmom.com. Heather has a passion to help stepmoms define their own positive path to success and focus on a peace filled heart rather than a perfect home. Heather brings faith based resources, encouragement and support to stepmoms while also speaking on divorce recovery, grace, forgiveness, healthy communication and remarriages in crisis.

She is the co-author of *Unwrapping The Gift of Stepfamily Peace*. Heather speaks and leads workshops for stepmothers at churches, conferences and community events. She also speaks with her husband, Andy, on the topic of remarriage and blending families to stepcouple audiences.

Her TV and radio broadcasts include:

- *Living the Word* with Glenn Mertz
- *Family Life Today* with Dennis Rainey and Bob Lepine
- *Inspiring Awesome* with James Carbary
- *Coparenting 101* with Deesha Philyaw
- *The Stepmom's Toolbox* with Peggy Nolan
- *MomLife Today*
- *Good Morning Cleveland*
- and more

Her magazine publications include:

- *Stepmom Magazine* (monthly contributor since 2010)

122

- *Praise and Coffee*
- *The Huffington Post*
- Various stepmom and Christian blogs for women

Heather is the cofounder of The Sisterhood of Stepmoms ministry. She speaks and leads workshops along with Laura and Gayla to encourage and support stepmothers bringing help, hope and healing to their hearts and to their homes.

Heather and her husband launched Learning2Step.com in 2015 to give stepcouples and their families access to resources, encouragement and support 24/7 to empower them on their journey.

Heather has contributed to the following books:

- *Co-parenting 101* by Deesha Philyaw
- *Stepping with Purpose* by Gayla Grace and Heather Hetchler
- *101 Tips for the Smart Stepmom* by Laura Petherbridge

Heather lives in Cleveland, OH with her husband, Andy, four children, and two stepchildren. She can be reached at www.CafeSmom.com.